BETTY CROCKER'S
Money-Saving Dinners

GOLDEN PRESS / NEW YORK
Western Publishing Company, Inc.
Racine, Wisconsin

Photography Director: George Ancona

Illustrator: Alice Golden

Second Printing, 1974

Library of Congress Catalog Card Number: 73-84540

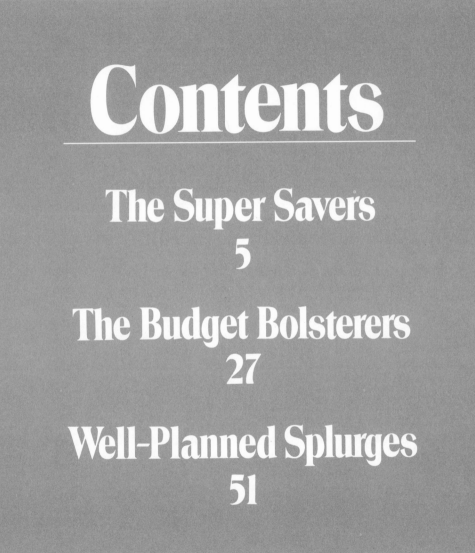

Contents

Dear Budget Watcher—

Let's face it. Clothes, cars, furniture, flowers—almost everything costs more than it used to. And while you can put off buying those luxuries for a time, there's no putting off the financial reality of the family dinner bill—and the chunk it's taking out of your already embattled budget. So the time has come to take a good, hard look at your food dollar—at what you're doing with it, and at what it's doing for you. Chances are, with these helpful tips and imaginative recipes—and a healthy sprinkling of your own common sense—you'll be able to get much more out of it.

Here, then, are four simple steps to help you spread your spending power:

1. Keep Informed. It's really up to you to be a knowledgeable consumer. Newspapers, magazines, food companies, government agencies—all offer the kind of information you need to keep up with these changing times. Be sure to note the "A Good Buy Word" paragraphs scattered through this book. Learn how to store and cook "budget foods." Find out about nutritional labeling and unit pricing. Read. Ask questions. And pass the information along to your friends and neighbors. Remember, everyone responds to and respects a well-informed consumer.

2. Plan Ahead. A reasonable, workable food budget begins with paper and pencil and informed preplanning. Plan your menus around nutritional guidelines (see the inside back cover) and advertised "specials," and do your shopping accordingly. Keep in mind your storage space, time schedule, food preferences and all those individual considerations that make your budget practical for you.

3. Shop Wisely. Stick to your shopping list. Buy only as much as your family will eat— or you can safely store. Read the labels. And remember that it's the cost per serving (not the price per ounce) that matters on the dinner table. Know what you're buying, price-wise and nutrition-wise.

4. Cook Creatively. Here's where the following pages play their part. You'll find a full month of budget-beating dinners, divided into three categories: The Super Savers, The Budget Bolsterers and Well-Planned Splurges. Let the state of your budget be your guide.

We hope this book will help you get more good food into your food budget. Look upon it as a challenge . . . and a chance for change.

Cordially,

Betty Crocker

1
The Super Savers

SOUP AND...
A CHANGE-OF-PACE
PROTEIN TO PUNCH
UP A DREARY DAY.

FOR EIGHT
Lentil Soup
Ham 'n Cheese Roll
Garden Salad
Fruit Freeze

LENTIL SOUP

2 cups lentils
3 slices bacon, cut into 2-inch pieces
1 clove garlic, finely chopped
1 medium onion, sliced
1 large carrot, sliced
1 large stalk celery, sliced
4 cups water

1 chicken bouillon cube
2 tablespoons snipped parsley
1 tablespoon salt
½ teaspoon pepper
1 bay leaf
¼ to ½ teaspoon thyme
1 can (28 ounces) whole tomatoes

Measure lentils into large saucepan or Dutch oven; cover with water. Heat to boiling; boil uncovered 2 minutes. Remove from heat; cover and let stand 1 hour.

Fry bacon until limp; remove and drain bacon. Add garlic, onion, carrot and celery to bacon fat remaining in skillet; cook and stir over medium-low heat until celery is tender and light brown, about 5 minutes. Stir into lentils. Stir in bacon and remaining ingredients except tomatoes. Heat to boiling. Reduce heat; cover and simmer 1 hour (soup will thicken). Stir in tomatoes (with liquid) and simmer uncovered 15 minutes. Remove bay leaf from soup before serving.

HAM 'N CHEESE ROLL

2 cups buttermilk baking mix
½ cup water
1 package (3 ounces) wafer-thin sliced cooked ham
1 cup shredded pasteurized process cheese spread loaf

1 can (4 ounces) mushroom stems and pieces, drained
⅓ cup chopped onion
Melted margarine

Heat oven to 400°. Stir baking mix and water until a soft dough forms. Smooth dough gently on floured cloth-covered board into a ball. Knead 5 times. Roll dough into rectangle, 12×8 inches. Layer ham on rectangle; sprinkle with cheese, mushrooms and onion. Roll up, beginning at narrow end. Cut into 1-inch slices. Fit slices into greased baking pan, 8×8×2 inches. Brush with margarine. Bake until golden brown, about 25 minutes.

GARDEN SALAD

4 cups finely shredded or chopped cabbage (about ½ medium)
¼ cup coarsely chopped green pepper
¼ cup coarsely chopped celery
¼ cup coarsely chopped turnip
¼ cup sliced radishes

1 tablespoon sliced green onion
½ cup unflavored yogurt
2 tablespoons vinegar
1 tablespoon sugar
½ teaspoon salt
Dash pepper

Measure vegetables into bowl; cover and refrigerate. Mix yogurt, vinegar, sugar, salt and pepper; cover and refrigerate. At serving time, toss yogurt dressing with vegetables.

FRUIT FREEZE

2 cups miniature marshmallows
1 cup orange juice or grape juice
2 tablespoons lemon juice

1 envelope (about 2 ounces) dessert topping mix

Heat marshmallows, juice and lemon juice over medium heat, stirring constantly, until marshmallows are melted and mixture is thick and syrupy, about 5 minutes. Cool.

Prepare topping mix as directed on package. Fold marshmallow mixture into topping. Pour into refrigerator tray. Freeze until firm, about 6 hours.

A GOOD-BUY WORD

Get your protein at penny prices. Count on dry beans, peas or lentils to come to the rescue as good, low-cost meat substitutes. If paired with a food of animal origin (such as eggs, cheese or milk—or even a tiny amount of meat), the protein value of these substitutes actually increases. Quite a nutritional equation!

GALA!
BAKED ALASKA PIE
ADDS THE PERFECT
FLOURISH TO THIS
GUEST-RIGHT MEAL.

FOR FOUR
Smoky Corn Puffs
**Spinach-Cucumber
Salad**
Alaska Peach Pie

SMOKY CORN PUFFS

Cornmeal Puffs (below)
Milk
1 can (8 ounces) whole kernel corn,
   drained (reserve liquid)
2 tablespoons margarine

2 tablespoons flour
½ teaspoon dry mustard
1 can (12 ounces) smoke-flavored pork
   luncheon meat, cut into ½-inch pieces
¼ cup thinly sliced green onion (with tops)

Bake Cornmeal Puffs. Add enough milk to reserved corn liquid to measure 1 cup. Melt margarine in medium saucepan over low heat. Stir in flour and mustard. Cook over low heat, stirring constantly, until mixture is smooth and bubbly. Remove from heat; stir in milk-corn liquid. Heat to boiling, stirring constantly. Boil and stir 1 minute. Stir in corn, meat and onion. Cook, stirring occasionally, until meat is hot, about 5 minutes.

Cut off tops of cool puffs. Pull out any filaments of soft dough. Fill puffs with hot filling and replace tops.

Variations

Chicken- or Ham-filled Corn Puffs: Substitute 2 cups cut-up cooked chicken or 2 cups diced cooked ham for the pork luncheon meat.

Cornmeal Puffs

½ cup water
¼ cup margarine
⅛ teaspoon salt

¼ cup yellow cornmeal
¼ cup all-purpose flour
2 eggs

Heat oven to 400°. Heat water, margarine and salt to rolling boil in medium saucepan. Stir in cornmeal and flour. Stir vigorously over low heat just until mixture forms a ball, about 1 minute. Remove from heat. Beat in eggs until smooth.

Drop dough by ¼ cupfuls onto ungreased baking sheet. Bake until puffed and golden, 35 to 40 minutes. Cool away from draft.

SPINACH-CUCUMBER SALAD

4 ounces spinach
2 medium cucumbers
¼ cup salad oil
1 tablespoon sugar

1 tablespoon vinegar
1 teaspoon soy sauce
¼ teaspoon dry mustard
⅛ teaspoon garlic powder

Tear spinach leaves into bite-size pieces (about 4 cups); refrigerate 1 hour. Place spinach in large bowl. Slice unpared cucumbers into bowl. Shake remaining ingredients in tightly covered jar; toss with vegetables.

ALASKA PEACH PIE

8-inch baked pie shell
3 cups vanilla ice cream, softened
1 can (16 ounces) sliced peaches,
    drained and chopped
¼ teaspoon vanilla

¼ teaspoon almond extract
2 egg whites
⅛ teaspoon cream of tartar
¼ cup brown sugar (packed)

Bake pie shell. Place softened ice cream in chilled bowl. Quickly stir in peaches, vanilla and almond extract; spoon into pie shell. Freeze until firm, at least 6 hours.

In small mixer bowl, beat egg whites and cream of tartar until foamy. Beat in brown sugar, 1 tablespoon at a time; beat until stiff and glossy (do not underbeat). Spread egg white meringue on ice cream, carefully sealing meringue to edge of crust. (Pie can be frozen up to 24 hours at this point.)

Heat oven to 500°. Bake until meringue is light brown, 3 to 5 minutes. Let stand 10 minutes before cutting.

A GOOD-BUY WORD

When it comes to shopping for fresh vegetables, take your cue from the season. When nature is bountiful, costs will be lower and quality will be higher. But buy only what you can use quickly or freeze, as most vegetables are rather perishable.

But what of canned vegetables? Although the food companies may do the picking and packing, the choosing is still up to you. Remember these pointers:

• Whole vegetables cost more than cut-up or pieces.

• You pay extra for fancy slices or seasonings.

• Know your grades: "A," or "Fancy," may be costlier but it has the same food value as its lower-graded counterparts.

ENCORE!
AN ELEGANT WRAP
FOR YESTERDAY'S
TURKEY STARS IN
THIS THOROUGHLY
SATISFYING MENU.

FOR FOUR
Turkey Crêpes
Chopped Broccoli
Romaine Salad
Cherry Pears

TURKEY CREPES

Crêpes (below)
3 tablespoons margarine
3 tablespoons flour
½ teaspoon salt
2 cups turkey or chicken broth*
2 cups finely cut-up turkey (see note)

½ cup chopped unpared apple
¼ cup chopped celery
2 tablespoons chopped onion
½ cup shredded pasteurized process
   cheese spread loaf

Prepare Crêpes. Keep crêpes covered to prevent them from drying out.

Melt margarine in medium saucepan over low heat. Stir in flour and salt. Cook over low heat, stirring constantly, until mixture is smooth and bubbly. Remove from heat; stir in broth. Heat to boiling, stirring constantly. Boil and stir 1 minute.

Heat oven to 350°. Mix turkey, apple, celery, onion and 1 cup of the thickened broth. Place about ¼ cup filling on center of each crêpe; roll up. Place seam side down in ungreased baking dish, 13½×9×2 inches. Pour remaining broth over crêpes. Sprinkle cheese on top. Bake uncovered until crêpes are hot and cheese is melted, about 20 minutes.

If using chicken bouillon cubes or instant bouillon for the broth, omit the salt.

Note: A 2-pound turkey leg will yield 2 cups cut-up cooked turkey. Cut the thigh from the leg. Place both pieces in large saucepan and add just enough water to cover. Season with 1 stalk celery, cut up; 1 medium carrot, sliced; 1 small onion, sliced; 2 teaspoons salt; ¼ teaspoon pepper. Heat to boiling. Reduce heat; cover and simmer until pieces are tender, about 2 hours. Refrigerate in broth. Remove meat from bones and skin and cut up. Reserve 2 cups of the turkey broth and use as directed in recipe.

Crêpes

1 cup all-purpose flour*
¼ teaspoon baking powder
¼ teaspoon salt

1¼ cups milk
1 egg
1 tablespoon margarine, melted

Beat all ingredients with rotary beater until smooth. For each crêpe, lightly grease 7- or 8-inch skillet with margarine; heat over medium heat until margarine is bubbly. Pour scant ¼ cup batter into skillet; immediately rotate pan until batter covers bottom. Cook until light brown; turn and brown. When removing from skillet, stack crêpes so first baked side is down.   12 crêpes.

If using self-rising flour, omit baking powder and salt.

ROMAINE SALAD

1 head romaine, torn into bite-size pieces (about 4 cups)
¼ cup sliced radishes
¼ cup salad oil
1 tablespoon cider vinegar
⅛ teaspoon onion salt
¼ teaspoon salt
½ teaspoon snipped parsley
1 tablespoon finely chopped green pepper
3 drops red pepper sauce
½ cup croutons (see note)

Mix romaine and sliced radishes in large bowl. Shake remaining ingredients except croutons in tightly covered jar; toss dressing with vegetables. Top with croutons.

Note: To make croutons, cut 1 slice white bread into ½-inch cubes and place on ungreased baking sheet. Bake in 300° oven, stirring frequently, until crisp and golden brown, about 20 minutes.

CHERRY PEARS

1½ cups vitamin C-enriched cherry-flavored drink
4 medium pears, pared and cut into halves
4 whole cloves
1 tablespoon cornstarch
1 tablespoon water

Heat cherry-flavored drink to boiling. Add pears and cloves. Reduce heat; cover and simmer, turning occasionally to color pears evenly, until pears are tender, about 20 minutes. Place pears in 4 dessert dishes; remove cloves.

Mix cornstarch and water; gradually stir into cherry drink. Cook, stirring constantly, until mixture thickens and boils. Boil and stir 1 minute. Spoon sauce onto pears. Cool to room temperature. Garnish with a dollop of whipped topping if you like.

PIZZAZZ!
A FRANKLY AMERICAN
FILLIP TOPS THE
HOMEMADE FIXINGS
FOR EVERYBODY'S
FAVORITE PIE.

FOR FOUR
Cheese-Frank Pizza
Antipasto Vegetables
Lime-Light

CHEESE-FRANK PIZZA

1 package active dry yeast
1 cup warm water (105 to 115°)
1 teaspoon sugar
1 teaspoon salt
2 tablespoons salad oil
2¾ to 3¼ cups all-purpose flour
Pizza Sauce (below)
1½ cups shredded mozzarella cheese*

1 cup chopped onion
1 can (4½ ounces) chopped ripe olives
   (optional)
1 cup chopped green pepper (optional)
1 can (4 ounces) mushroom stems
   and pieces (optional)
6 frankfurters, sliced, or 4 ounces
   sliced pepperoni

In large bowl, dissolve yeast in warm water. Stir in sugar, salt, oil and 2¼ cups of the flour; beat until smooth. Turn dough onto floured surface. Knead in enough remaining flour to make dough easy to handle; knead until smooth, 2 to 5 minutes. Place in greased bowl; turn greased side up. Cover and let rise in warm place until double, about 45 minutes.

Prepare Pizza Sauce; set aside.

Heat oven to 400°. Punch down dough; divide in half. Roll each half on lightly floured surface into 12-inch circle. Place on ungreased baking sheet. Spoon half the sauce on each circle; spread evenly to outer edge. Sprinkle each circle with ½ cup cheese; top each with half the vegetables (drained if necessary) and meat. Sprinkle each pizza with ¼ cup remaining cheese. Bake one pizza at a time on center rack of oven 25 minutes. Use kitchen scissors to cut pizzas easily.

You can substitute 1½ cups shredded pasteurized process cheese spread loaf for the mozzarella cheese. Do not sprinkle cheese spread on pizza before baking. Bake pizza 20 minutes, then sprinkle cheese on top and bake until cheese is melted and bubbly, about 5 minutes.

Pizza Sauce

1 can (6 ounces) tomato paste
½ cup water
1 teaspoon salt
1 teaspoon oregano
¼ teaspoon thyme

¼ teaspoon marjoram
¼ teaspoon garlic salt
⅛ teaspoon pepper
Dash red pepper sauce

Mix all ingredients thoroughly.

ANTIPASTO VEGETABLES

Marinade (below)
1 carrot, cut into julienne strips
1 parsnip, cut into ⅛-inch slices
1 large stalk celery, cut into
   julienne strips

3 radishes
Crisp lettuce leaves

Prepare Marinade. Add carrot, parsnip and celery to jar of marinade. Cover and shake until vegetables are coated. Refrigerate at least 2 hours (no longer than 24 hours). Just before serving, drain vegetables and place in bowl. Slice radishes thinly into bowl; toss. Serve on lettuce.

Marinade

¼ cup vinegar
¼ cup salad oil
½ teaspoon salt
½ teaspoon rosemary leaves

½ teaspoon parsley flakes
¼ teaspoon red pepper sauce
¼ teaspoon prepared mustard
⅛ teaspoon sugar

Shake all ingredients in tightly covered wide-mouth quart jar.

LIME-LIGHT

1 package (3 ounces) lime-flavored
   gelatin

1½ cups vanilla ice cream,
   softened

Prepare gelatin as directed on package except—refrigerate until slightly thickened but not set. Beat with electric mixer on medium speed ½ minute. Beat in ice cream on low speed. Beat on medium-high speed 1½ minutes. Pour into 4 dessert dishes. Cover and refrigerate until set, about 4 hours. Garnish with whipped cream and maraschino cherries if you like.

SALMON FRITTERS

1 can (16 ounces) salmon, drained
  and flaked
1 cup buttermilk baking mix
1 egg
½ teaspoon salt

1 tablespoon lemon juice
2 tablespoons sliced green onion
  (with tops)
2 tablespoons finely chopped green pepper
1 teaspoon dill weed

In deep fat fryer or kettle, heat 3 to 4 inches fat or oil to 365°.

Mix all ingredients; drop by rounded teaspoonfuls, a few at a time, into hot fat. Fry, turning once, until golden brown, about 2 minutes. Drain.   About 24 fritters.

POPPY SEED BEANS

1 can (16 ounces) French-style green
  beans
½ teaspoon poppy seed

3 or 4 drops red pepper sauce
1 tablespoon margarine

Heat beans (with liquid); drain. Sprinkle with poppy seed and red pepper sauce; dot with margarine and toss.

PEAS 'N CARROT SALAD

1 cup boiling water
1 package (3 ounces) lemon-flavored
  gelatin
½ teaspoon salt
1 can (8 ounces) peas and carrots,
  drained (reserve liquid)

1 tablespoon vinegar
2 teaspoons grated onion
½ cup chopped celery

Pour boiling water onto gelatin and salt in bowl; stir until gelatin is dissolved. Add enough water to reserved vegetable liquid to measure ¾ cup; stir vegetable liquid, vinegar and onion into gelatin. Refrigerate until slightly thickened but not set.

Stir in peas and carrots and celery. Pour into 4-cup mold. Cover and refrigerate until firm, at least 4 hours.

GINGERBREAD WITH ORANGE SAUCE

Bake 1 package (14.5 ounces) gingerbread mix as directed. Cool slightly. Cut gingerbread in half; reserve one half for future use (see note). Cut remaining half into 4 pieces. Top each piece with a teaspoonful of Hard Sauce (below). Spoon Orange Sauce (below) over each serving.

Hard Sauce

2 tablespoons margarine, softened   ½ teaspoon vanilla
¼ cup confectioners' sugar

Mix all ingredients until smooth. Refrigerate at least 1 hour.

Orange Sauce

½ teaspoon cornstarch   1 teaspoon honey
1 can (11 ounces) mandarin orange   2 tablespoons raisins
   segments, drained (reserve syrup)

Mix cornstarch and reserved orange syrup in small saucepan; stir in honey. Cook over medium heat, stirring constantly, until sauce thickens and boils. Boil and stir 1 minute. Carefully stir in orange segments and raisins. Serve warm or chilled.

Note: Call on gingerbread for a change-of-pace breakfast dish. Wrap in aluminum foil and heat in 350° oven until warm, about 20 minutes. Serve in bowls and top with milk and sliced bananas.

A GOOD-BUY WORD

When it comes to canned salmon, color can be a costly commodity. In general, the redder the flesh, the higher the price. So, while you'd be right in choosing the more expensive salmon for salads, opt for the lower-priced varieties for fritters and casseroles, when color matters not.

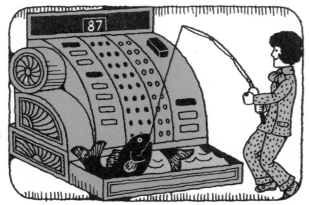

DRESS-UP . . .
PUT A NEW FACE ON
AN EVERYDAY FOOD
AND WATCH THOSE
SMILES COME ON.

FOR SIX
Cottage-Egg Salad
Chili Tomatoes
Sesame Melba Triangles
Melon Pie

COTTAGE-EGG SALAD

1 cup boiling water
1 package (3 ounces) lemon-flavored
   gelatin
1 teaspoon salt
1 cup cold water
9 hard-cooked eggs, cut crosswise in half

1 medium cucumber, shredded and well
   drained
1 tablespoon grated onion
1½ cups creamed cottage cheese
½ teaspoon tarragon leaves, crushed
5 drops red pepper sauce

Pour boiling water onto gelatin and salt in large bowl; stir until gelatin is dissolved. Stir in cold water. Refrigerate until mixture is slightly thickened but not set.

Spread 1 cup of the gelatin in baking dish, 11¾ × 7½ × 1¾ inches. Gently press eggs, cut sides down, into gelatin.

Beat remaining gelatin until light and fluffy; stir in remaining ingredients. Pour gelatin mixture over eggs. Cover and refrigerate until firm, at least 8 hours.

CHILI TOMATOES

4 tomatoes, cut into ¼-inch slices
1 large green pepper, cut into thin rings
¼ cup salad oil
2 tablespoons vinegar

½ teaspoon salt
⅛ teaspoon garlic powder
1 tablespoon chili sauce
Crisp lettuce leaves

Layer tomato slices and green pepper rings in shallow glass dish. Shake remaining ingredients except lettuce in tightly covered jar; pour onto vegetables. Cover and refrigerate at least 4 hours. To serve, drain vegetables and arrange on lettuce leaves.

SESAME MELBA TRIANGLES

Unsliced loaf of bread
2 tablespoons soft margarine

¼ teaspoon salt
1 tablespoon sesame seed

Heat oven to 350°. Cut nine ¼-inch slices from loaf of bread; remove crusts. Mix remaining ingredients and spread evenly on slices. Cut each slice diagonally in half; place on ungreased baking sheet. Bake until crisp and golden brown, about 20 minutes.   18 triangles.

MELON PIE

Pastry for 9-inch Two-crust Pie (below)
½ cup sugar
⅓ cup all-purpose flour
½ teaspoon pumpkin pie spice
4 cups sliced pared cantaloupe
  (about 1 medium)

1 tablespoon lime juice
2 tablespoons margarine
1 teaspoon sugar
Vanilla ice cream

Heat oven to 425°. Prepare pastry. Mix ½ cup sugar, the flour and pumpkin pie spice; toss with cantaloupe slices. Turn into pastry-lined pie pan; sprinkle with lime juice and dot with margarine.

Cover with top crust which has slits cut in it; seal and flute. Sprinkle crust with 1 teaspoon sugar. Cover edge with 2- to 3-inch strip of aluminum foil to prevent excessive browning; remove foil for the last 15 minutes of baking. Bake until crust is golden brown and juice begins to bubble through slits, 40 to 50 minutes. Serve warm, with ice cream.

Pastry for 9-inch Two-crust Pie

2 cups all-purpose flour*
1 teaspoon salt

⅔ cup plus 2 tablespoons shortening
4 or 5 tablespoons cold water

Measure flour and salt into bowl. Cut in shortening thoroughly. Sprinkle in water, 1 tablespoon at a time, mixing until all flour is moistened and dough almost cleans side of bowl (1 to 2 teaspoons water can be added if needed).

Gather dough into a ball; divide in half. Shape on lightly floured cloth-covered board into 2 flattened rounds. Roll one round 2 inches larger than inverted pie pan. Fold pastry into quarters; unfold and ease into pan.

Turn filling into pastry-lined pie pan. Trim overhanging edge of pastry ½ inch from rim of pan.

Roll second round of dough. Fold into quarters; cut slits so steam can escape. Place over filling and unfold. Trim overhanging edge of pastry 1 inch from rim of pan. Fold and roll top edge under lower edge, pressing on rim to seal; flute.

* If using self-rising flour, omit salt. Pie crusts made with self-rising flour differ in flavor and texture from those made with plain flour.

5
STARS—
A SPECIAL SLANT
ON A SKINFLINT
STAPLE LEADS THE
WAY TO A WINNER
OF A DINNER.

· FOR FOUR
Real Winner Liver
Golden Glow Noodles
Vegetable Marinade
Banana-Orange Mix

REAL WINNER LIVER

½ cup salad oil
⅓ cup all-purpose flour
1 teaspoon salt
⅛ teaspoon pepper
1½ pounds sliced beef liver
   (¼ to ½ inch thick)

2 eggs, beaten
1½ cups cracker crumbs (about 36 crackers)
1 cup water
1 beef bouillon cube
1 tablespoon margarine
1 teaspoon lemon juice

Heat oil in large skillet. Mix flour, salt and pepper. Coat meat with flour mixture, then dip into beaten eggs and coat with cracker crumbs. Brown meat in oil over medium-high heat, about 3 minutes on each side. Remove meat from skillet. Drain meat and place on warm serving platter; keep warm in 200° oven.

Drain fat from skillet. In same skillet, heat water and bouillon cube to boiling. Reduce heat; simmer 5 minutes, stirring occasionally. Remove from heat; stir in margarine and lemon juice. Serve with liver.

GOLDEN GLOW NOODLES

2 eggs
2 tablespoons milk
1 teaspoon salt
1½ cups all-purpose flour
3 quarts water

1 tablespoon salt
1 tablespoon salad oil
Cheese Sauce (right)
1 tablespoon snipped parsley

Beat eggs until foamy. Mix in milk, 1 teaspoon salt and the flour. Knead dough in bowl to form a ball. Turn dough onto lightly floured cloth-covered board. Knead until very smooth, about 1 minute. Cover and let rest 30 minutes.

Divide dough into 4 equal parts. Roll each part on floured surface into 12-inch circle. (Keep remaining dough covered until ready to roll.) Let circles stand uncovered 15 minutes to dry.

In Dutch oven or kettle, heat water, 1 tablespoon salt and the oil to boiling. Stack circles and cut into ¼-inch strips. Cook strips in boiling water until tender, about 15 minutes.

While noodles are cooking, prepare Cheese Sauce. Drain noodles and fold into sauce. Garnish with parsley.

Cheese Sauce

2 tablespoons margarine
2 tablespoons flour
¼ teaspoon salt

1 cup milk
⅓ cup shredded pasteurized process
    cheese spread loaf

Melt margarine in medium saucepan over low heat. Stir in flour and salt. Cook over low heat, stirring constantly, until mixture is smooth and bubbly. Remove from heat. Stir in milk. Heat to boiling, stirring constantly. Boil and stir 1 minute. Remove from heat; stir in cheese spread. Stir until cheese is melted and sauce is smooth.

VEGETABLE MARINADE

1 can (16 ounces) sliced carrots, drained
1 can (16 ounces) cut green beans, drained
1 small onion, sliced and separated
    into rings
2 tablespoons chopped celery

¼ cup vinegar
2 tablespoons sugar
1 tablespoon salad oil
½ teaspoon salt
½ teaspoon dry mustard

Place carrots and beans in separate sections of shallow glass dish, about 10×6 inches. Arrange onion rings on carrots and beans; sprinkle with celery. Shake remaining ingredients in tightly covered jar; pour over vegetables. Cover and refrigerate at least 2 hours. Drain before serving.

BANANA-ORANGE MIX

2 medium oranges, chilled
2 medium bananas

¼ cup flaked coconut

Pare and section oranges. Peel bananas and cut into ¼-inch slices. Toss fruits with coconut.

A GOOD-BUY WORD

Looking for a servings stretcher? Look to rice. Or macaroni. Or noodles or spaghetti. Perfect go-withs for any main course. Ideal in-withs for casseroles. They not only help to make your meat go farther, but ½ cup also counts as one of your four daily servings of "Breads and Cereals." Read the package information carefully—and let the price *per serving* (rather than the price per ounce) determine your choice.

1

, 2, 3...

IT'S AS EASY AS THAT WITH A MEAL PLAN LIKE THIS.

FOR SIX
Hamburger Potpourri
Lettuce Wedges with Yogurt Dressing
Crackers or Breadsticks
Cranberry Freeze

HAMBURGER POTPOURRI

1½ **pounds ground beef**
⅔ **cup chopped onion**
1 **clove garlic, crushed**
2 **cans (10¾ ounces each) condensed vegetable soup**
1 **can (16 ounces) pork and beans in tomato sauce**

3 **cups water**
⅔ **cup chopped celery**
1¼ **teaspoons salt**
1 **teaspoon oregano leaves**
½ **teaspoon Worcestershire sauce**
¼ **teaspoon basil leaves**
¼ **teaspoon fennel seed**

Cook and stir meat, onion and garlic in large saucepan or Dutch oven until meat is brown and onion is tender. Drain off fat. Stir in remaining ingredients. Heat to boiling. Reduce heat; cover and simmer 20 minutes.

LETTUCE WEDGES WITH YOGURT DRESSING

1 **cup unflavored yogurt**
½ **cup chopped cucumber**
1 **tablespoon sugar**

⅛ **teaspoon dill weed**
Dash salt
1 **head lettuce, cut into 6 wedges**

Mix all ingredients except lettuce in small bowl. Serve on lettuce wedges.

CRANBERRY FREEZE

Mix 1 can (16 ounces) whole cranberry sauce and 1 cup club soda. Pour into refrigerator tray; freeze until mushy and partially frozen, 30 to 60 minutes. Turn into chilled large bowl; beat until smooth and pink. Pour into refrigerator tray; freeze until firm, about 6 hours. Let stand at room temperature about 30 minutes before serving.   4 to 6 servings.

A GOOD-BUY WORD

Hamburger is hamburger. Right? Wrong! The cheapest grind—usually labeled hamburger or regular ground beef—contains a variety of beef cuts. It also contains more fat. But that's fine for a juicy patty. And it's fine for a main dish too—if you drain the meat. The leaner types of ground beef (ground chuck or ground round) come from beef cuts that are often in demand. They have less fat, true—but a higher price tag. It all broils down to a matter of personal preference—and several pennies more per pound.

P. S. Keep an eye out for ground beef supplemented with vegetable protein sources—it may be your best bargain by far.

KRAUT 'N SAUSAGE RING

2 pounds bulk pork sausage
1⅓ cups soft bread crumbs
2 eggs, slightly beaten
1⅓ cups finely chopped apple
⅓ cup minced onion

½ teaspoon cinnamon
⅛ teaspoon cloves
1 can (28.5 ounces) sauerkraut
1 teaspoon caraway seed

Heat oven to 350°. Mix sausage, bread crumbs, eggs, apple, onion, cinnamon and cloves. Press lightly into ungreased 6-cup ring mold. Unmold sausage mixture onto rack in shallow baking pan; cover loosely with aluminum foil. Bake 30 minutes. Remove foil; bake 30 minutes longer.

While ring is baking, heat sauerkraut (with liquid) and caraway seed, stirring occasionally; drain. Using wide spatulas, remove sausage ring to warm serving platter; spoon sauerkraut into center.

APPLE-PEPPER JELLY

1 jar (10 ounces) apple jelly
1 tablespoon crushed red peppers

6 drops red food color

Heat jelly and peppers to boiling, stirring constantly. Stir in food color. Strain into jar; refrigerate. Serve with meat. Store leftover jelly in refrigerator.

BUTTERED GREEN BEANS WITH RADISHES

2 packages (9 ounces each) frozen cut
    green beans
1 tablespoon margarine

2 radishes, thinly sliced
Salt and pepper

Cook beans as directed on package; drain. Toss beans with margarine and radishes. Season with salt and pepper.

SHAPE-UP! RING AROUND THE SAUERKRAUT! WHAT FASHIONABLE FORM FOR SAUSAGE.

FOR SIX
Kraut 'n Sausage Ring
Apple-Pepper Jelly
Buttered Green Beans
with Radishes
Cheese-crusted Loaves
Easy Freeze Fruit

CHEESE-CRUSTED LOAVES

1 loaf (1 pound) frozen bread dough
Shortening
Cornmeal

About ¼ cup cheese-flavored cracker crumbs

Heat oven to 200°; turn off. Place baking pan, 8×8×2 inches, on bottom rack in oven; pour in boiling water to ½-inch depth. Rub frozen loaf with shortening; place in greased loaf pan, 9×5×3 inches, and place in oven (on rack above pan of water) to thaw 1 hour.

Sprinkle ungreased baking sheet with cornmeal. Remove loaf from pan; cut into 6 equal pieces. Shape each piece into a miniature loaf, about 3×1½ inches. Roll top of each loaf in cracker crumbs and place on baking sheet. Sprinkle tops and sides of loaves with cold water; let rise at room temperature 30 minutes.

Heat oven to 350°. Place baking pan, 8×8×2 inches, on bottom rack in oven; pour in boiling water to ½-inch depth. Sprinkle loaves with cold water; sprinkle each with about 1 teaspoon cracker crumbs. Bake until crust is set and golden brown, about 35 minutes.

EASY FREEZE FRUIT

1 cup miniature marshmallows
1 can (8¼ ounces) crushed pineapple
1 can (16 ounces) fruit cocktail, drained
⅓ cup nonfat dry milk

¼ cup iced water
2 teaspoons lemon juice
2 teaspoons vanilla
2 tablespoons sugar

Mix marshmallows and pineapple (with syrup); let stand at room temperature about 4 hours, stirring occasionally.

Stir in fruit cocktail. In small mixer bowl, beat dry milk and iced water on high speed until stiff peaks form, about 5 minutes. Mix in lemon juice, vanilla and sugar; fold into marshmallow-pineapple mixture. Spread in refrigerator tray; cover with aluminum foil. Freeze at least 6 hours. To serve, cut into cubes and pile into 6 sherbet dishes. For a company air, pour grenadine or crème de menthe over cubes.

CANNELLONI

Pasta Squares (below)
1 pound ground beef
3 chicken livers, chopped
¼ cup chopped onion
1 clove garlic, finely chopped
1 egg
2 tablespoons milk

2 tablespoons snipped parsley
1 teaspoon salt
½ teaspoon oregano leaves
Sauce (page 26)
1 package (4 ounces) shredded mozzarella cheese

Prepare Pasta Squares. Cook and stir ground beef over medium heat until brown. Drain off fat, reserving 1 tablespoon. Remove meat to medium bowl. Return reserved fat to skillet. Add livers, onion and garlic; cook and stir until onion is tender and liver is light brown, 3 to 4 minutes. Turn liver mixture into bowl with meat. Mix in egg, milk, parsley, salt and oregano.

Prepare Sauce. Place about 1 tablespoon meat mixture on each pasta square. Roll up; place seam side down in single layer in greased baking dish, 13½ × 9 × 2 inches. Spoon Sauce over rolls; sprinkle with cheese. (At this point, casserole can be covered and refrigerated up to 24 hours.)

Heat oven to 375°. Bake uncovered until hot and bubbly, about 40 minutes.

Pasta Squares

2 eggs
3 tablespoons milk

1 teaspoon salt
1½ cups all-purpose flour

Beat eggs until foamy. Mix in milk, salt and flour until dough cleans side of bowl. Press dough into a ball and turn onto floured board. Knead until dough loses stickiness and becomes smooth, about 2 minutes. Cover and let rest 30 minutes.

Divide dough in half. Roll one half at a time on well-floured board into 16-inch square—dough will be paper-thin. (Keep remaining dough covered until ready to roll.) Cut into sixteen 4-inch squares. Let squares stand uncovered 20 minutes to dry.

Heat 3 quarts water and 1 tablespoon salt to boiling. Cook squares in boiling water, stirring occasionally, until tender, 10 to 12 minutes. Drain; rinse under running cold water. Spread squares on paper towels to dry.

PAYOFF—
CASH IN ON A GOOD THING WITH A BASIC ITALIAN DOUGH.
MOLTO BENE!

FOR SIX
Cannelloni
Italian Breadsticks
Stir-fried Zucchini
and Carrots
Peppermint Cups

Sauce

1 can (16 ounces) whole tomatoes	1 teaspoon sugar
1 can (6 ounces) tomato paste	½ teaspoon salt
1 cup water	¼ teaspoon basil
1 clove garlic, finely chopped	¼ teaspoon oregano leaves
2 tablespoons chopped onion	Dash pepper

Place all ingredients in saucepan; break up tomatoes with a fork. Heat to boiling, stirring occasionally. Reduce heat; simmer uncovered 15 minutes.

STIR-FRIED ZUCCHINI AND CARROTS

3 tablespoons salad oil	Dash pepper
4 medium zucchini, cubed	¾ cup shredded pasteurized process
4 large carrots, thinly sliced	cheese spread loaf
¼ teaspoon salt	

Heat oil in large skillet over medium heat. Add zucchini and carrots; cook and stir just until crisp-tender, 3 to 4 minutes. Stir in salt, pepper and cheese spread. Heat, stirring constantly, until cheese is melted and vegetables are coated.

PEPPERMINT CUPS

1 package (6 ounces) semisweet chocolate pieces	1 pint vanilla ice cream
1 tablespoon shortening	¼ teaspoon peppermint extract
	3 drops red or green food color

Melt chocolate pieces and shortening over medium heat, stirring frequently, until smooth, 3 to 4 minutes. Cool.

Line 6 medium muffin cups with paper baking cups. Place 1 tablespoon melted chocolate in each cup; press against side of cup with the back of a spoon. Refrigerate until firm. Fill in with remaining chocolate.

Remove paper baking cups from chocolate molds. Soften ice cream slightly in chilled bowl; stir in peppermint extract and food color. Divide among chocolate molds. Serve immediately.

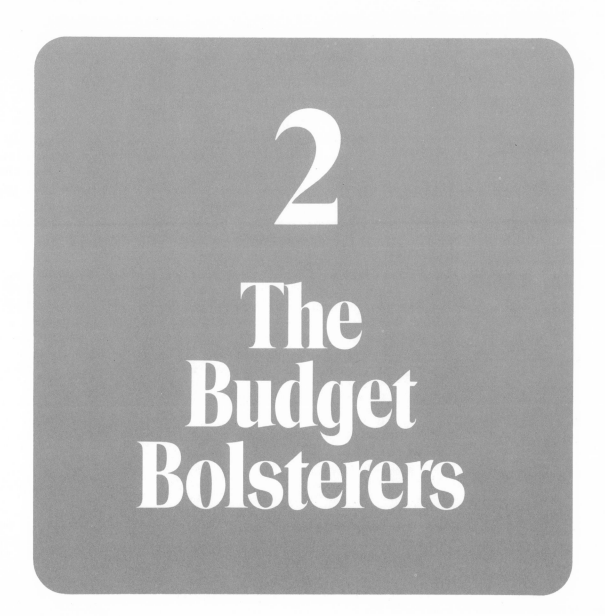

2

The
Budget
Bolsterers

SHIPSHAPE!
KEEP YOUR EYE OUT
FOR SAVING SALES
AND TRIM THOSE GOOD
BUYS WITH STYLE.

FOR FOUR
Fish Stick Casserole
Zucchini-Tomato
Combo
Lemon-buttered
English Muffins
Apple-Raisin Topover

FISH STICK CASSEROLE

4 medium potatoes (about 1⅓ pounds) *
1 package (14 ounces) frozen breaded
   fish sticks
2 tablespoons lemon juice
1 cup unflavored yogurt
1½ cups shredded pasteurized process
   cheese spread loaf

¼ cup milk
¼ cup chopped green onion (with tops)
1 teaspoon salt
¼ teaspoon pepper
3 slices bacon, crisply fried and crumbled

Heat 1 inch salted water (½ teaspoon salt to 1 cup water) to boiling in saucepan. Add unpared potatoes; cover and heat to boiling. Reduce heat; simmer until tender, 30 to 35 minutes. Drain potatoes and peel.

While potatoes are cooking, heat oven to 450°. Arrange frozen fish sticks on ungreased baking sheet. Bake until fish sticks are just crisp, 15 to 20 minutes. Cool and brush with lemon juice.

Reduce oven temperature to 350°. Mix yogurt, cheese, milk, onion, salt and pepper. Cut potatoes into thin slices; fold into yogurt-cheese mixture. Place fish sticks upright around inner edge of greased 1½-quart casserole. Turn potato mixture into casserole; sprinkle with bacon. Cover loosely with aluminum foil. Bake 25 minutes; remove foil. Bake until potato mixture is bubbly and fish sticks are golden brown, about 20 minutes longer. (If fish sticks brown before potatoes are bubbly, cover the tips loosely with foil.)

* *Potatoes should be moist and waxy, about 3×2 inches in size.*

ZUCCHINI-TOMATO COMBO

1 medium onion, sliced
1 clove garlic, finely chopped
2 tablespoons salad oil
1 pound zucchini (about 4 small), * cut into
   ½-inch slices
1 can (16 ounces) whole tomatoes

½ teaspoon salt
¼ teaspoon oregano
Dash pepper
2 teaspoons cornstarch
1 tablespoon water

In large skillet, cook and stir onion and garlic in oil over medium heat until tender, about 3 minutes. Add zucchini; cook, stirring frequently, until zucchini is crisp-tender, about 4 minutes. Stir in tomatoes (with liquid), salt, oregano and pepper; simmer uncovered 10 minutes. Mix cornstarch and water;

stir into tomato mixture. Cook over medium heat, stirring constantly, until mixture thickens and boils, about 1 minute.

* You can substitute 1 can (16 ounces) zucchini for the fresh zucchini.

LEMON-BUTTERED ENGLISH MUFFINS

¼ cup margarine, softened
1 tablespoon honey

½ teaspoon grated lemon peel
4 to 6 English muffins, split

In small mixer bowl, beat margarine, honey and lemon peel on medium speed until fluffy, about 2 minutes, scraping bowl frequently. Toast muffin halves; spread lemon butter on hot muffins.   4 to 6 servings.

APPLE-RAISIN TOPOVER

2 apples, pared and thinly sliced
½ cup raisins
¼ cup chopped nuts
⅓ cup brown sugar (packed)
1¼ cups all-purpose flour*
1 cup granulated sugar
¾ teaspoon soda
¾ teaspoon salt

⅛ teaspoon baking powder
½ teaspoon cinnamon
¼ teaspoon cloves
¼ teaspoon allspice
¾ cup applesauce
¼ cup water
¼ cup shortening
1 egg

Heat oven to 350°. Mix apple slices, raisins, nuts and brown sugar; spread in buttered baking pan, 9×9×2 inches.

Measure remaining ingredients into large mixer bowl. Blend on low speed ½ minute, scraping bowl constantly. Beat on high speed 3 minutes, scraping bowl occasionally. Pour over fruit in pan. Bake until a wooden pick inserted in center comes out clean, 50 to 60 minutes. Invert onto serving plate; cut into 9 squares. Serve with whipped topping if you like.

* Do not use self-rising flour in this recipe.

FOR SIX
Midwestern Meat Loaves
Snappy Sweet Potatoes
Spinach Salad
Pineapple Pompons

MIDWESTERN MEAT LOAVES

1 can (5⅓ ounces) evaporated milk	2 pounds ground beef
1 egg	⅓ cup chopped onion
2 tablespoons catsup	1½ teaspoons salt
¼ teaspoon red pepper sauce	¼ teaspoon thyme or marjoram
1½ cups soft bread crumbs (about 5 slices)	

Beat milk, egg, catsup and red pepper sauce in large bowl. Mix in remaining ingredients. Shape mixture into 6 miniature loaves (about ¾ cup per loaf). Place on rack in ungreased baking pan, 13×9×2 inches. Bake in 350° oven 30 to 35 minutes. Garnish with dill pickle slices or onion rings.

SNAPPY SWEET POTATOES

1 tablespoon orange instant soft drink mix	1 can (18 ounces) vacuum-pack sweet potatoes*
1 tablespoon cornstarch	1 can (16 ounces) sliced peaches, drained
⅓ cup brown sugar (packed)	1 teaspoon snipped parsley
3 tablespoons margarine	
½ cup water	

In 10-inch skillet, cook orange drink mix, cornstarch, brown sugar, margarine and water over medium heat, stirring constantly, until mixture thickens and boils, 3 to 5 minutes. Stir in sweet potatoes and peach slices. Reduce heat; cook, stirring gently, until glazed and hot. Sprinkle with parsley.

You can substitute 2 pounds sweet potatoes or yams (about 6 medium), cooked, for the canned sweet potatoes.

SPINACH SALAD

8 ounces spinach
¼ cup salad oil
2 tablespoons vinegar
1 small clove garlic, crushed
½ teaspoon salt

Dash pepper
1 small cucumber, thinly sliced
1 hard-cooked egg, chopped
2 slices bacon, crisply fried and crumbled

Tear spinach leaves into bite-size pieces (about 8 cups); refrigerate 1 hour. Shake oil, vinegar, garlic, salt and pepper in tightly covered jar; refrigerate at least 1 hour to blend flavors.

Just before serving, shake dressing; toss with spinach until leaves are well coated. Sprinkle with cucumber, egg and bacon; toss.

PINEAPPLE POMPONS

¼ cup sugar
¼ cup margarine
1 can (8¼ ounces) crushed pineapple,
   drained (reserve 1 tablespoon syrup)

2 tablespoons chopped nuts
18 vanilla wafers
3 cups frozen whipped topping (thawed)
¾ cup flaked coconut

Mix sugar and margarine. Stir in pineapple, reserved pineapple syrup and nuts. Stack 3 vanilla wafers so rounded sides are on bottom and top, spreading 1 level tablespoon pineapple filling between wafers. Stand upright in ungreased baking dish, 13½ × 9 × 2 inches. Repeat 5 times. Frost side and top of each stack with whipped topping. Sprinkle each stack with 2 tablespoons coconut. Refrigerate until serving time.

MAIS OUI!
A FRANCOPHILE'S
DELIGHT: A HEARTY
FISH STEW, CRUSTY
BREAD AND A LIGHT
CITRUS SOUFFLE.

FOR SIX
Budget Bouillabaisse
French Bread Puff
Orange Soufflé

BUDGET BOUILLABAISSE

2 tablespoons salad oil
1 cup chopped onion
½ cup chopped celery
2 cloves garlic, finely chopped
¼ teaspoon fennel seed
½ teaspoon thyme leaves
1 bay leaf
⅛ teaspoon cayenne red pepper
¼ teaspoon oregano leaves
½ teaspoon salt

1 tablespoon snipped parsley
1 can (28 ounces) whole tomatoes
1 teaspoon lemon juice
2 cans (10½ ounces each) condensed
    chicken broth
¼ cup cornstarch
1 cup water
2 pounds frozen cod, partially thawed
    and cut into 1-inch pieces

Heat oil in Dutch oven over medium heat. Add onion and celery; cook and stir until onion is tender and celery is crisp-tender, about 4 minutes. Stir in seasonings, parsley, tomatoes (with liquid) and lemon juice. Heat to boiling. Reduce heat; simmer uncovered 15 minutes. Remove bay leaf; stir in chicken broth.

Mix cornstarch and water; stir into broth mixture. Cook, stirring constantly, until mixture thickens and boils. Stir in fish. Simmer until fish is tender, about 10 minutes. Season with salt and pepper.

FRENCH BREAD PUFF

1 loaf (1 pound) French bread
½ cup margarine, softened
¼ teaspoon garlic powder
2 tablespoons finely chopped onion
    or snipped chives

2 eggs, separated
½ cup shredded pasteurized process cheese
    spread loaf
1 tablespoon snipped parsley

Heat oven to 350°. Cut bread into 1-inch slices. Mix margarine, garlic powder and onion; spread on slices. Reassemble loaf; wrap securely in aluminum foil, 28 × 12 inches. Place on ungreased baking sheet. Heat in oven 20 minutes.

While loaf is heating, beat egg whites until stiff. Beat egg yolks until thick and lemon colored. Fold egg yolks and cheese spread into egg whites. Remove loaf from oven; fold back foil and tuck down around base of loaf. Spoon egg mixture onto loaf; sprinkle with parsley. Bake until topping is a delicate golden brown, about 4 minutes.

ORANGE SOUFFLE

¼ cup sugar
¼ teaspoon salt
1 envelope unflavored gelatin
3 eggs, separated
1 cup water
3 to 4 tablespoons orange juice
1 teaspoon grated orange peel

2 drops each red and yellow food color (optional)
3 tablespoons sugar
1 container (10½ ounces) frozen whipped topping (thawed)
1 can (11 ounces) mandarin orange segments, drained

Mix ¼ cup sugar, the salt and gelatin in small saucepan. Beat egg yolks, water and orange juice; stir into sugar mixture. Cook over medium heat, stirring constantly, just until mixture boils. Remove from heat; stir in orange peel and food colors. Chill pan in bowl of ice and water or in refrigerator, stirring occasionally, until mixture mounds slightly when dropped from a spoon.

Beat egg whites until foamy. Beat in 3 tablespoons sugar, 1 tablespoon at a time; beat until stiff and glossy. Fold orange mixture into egg white meringue, then fold in topping and orange segments. Pour into ungreased 4-cup soufflé dish or 1-quart casserole. Refrigerate until set, at least 6 hours.

A GOOD-BUY WORD

Use the big blocks of process cheese spread whenever you can—it's the least expensive type of cheese by far. Like its costlier cousins, process cheese spread is a special blend of pasteurized cheeses, but it has less fat and more moisture. And that extra moisture makes it tops for recipes that call for melted cheese. Remember it for your main dishes, to be sure, but especially for appetizers and sandwiches.

FOR FOUR
Ham Soufflé
Fried Tomatoes
Relish Kabobs
Toasted Rye Bread
with Avocado Butter
Pumpkin Cookie-Cake

HAM SOUFFLE

¼ cup margarine
¼ cup all-purpose flour
¼ teaspoon salt
Dash pepper
¼ teaspoon prepared mustard
1 cup milk

1 cup cottage cheese (small curd)
1 can (4½ ounces) deviled ham spread
¼ cup chopped green onion (with tops)
4 eggs, separated
¼ teaspoon cream of tartar

Heat oven to 350°. Grease 6-cup soufflé dish or 1½-quart casserole.

Melt margarine in large saucepan over low heat. Mix in flour, salt, pepper and mustard. Cook over low heat, stirring constantly, until mixture is smooth and bubbly. Remove from heat. Stir in milk. Heat to boiling, stirring constantly. Boil and stir 1 minute. Remove from heat. Stir in cottage cheese, deviled ham and green onion.

Beat egg whites and cream of tartar until stiff but not dry. Beat egg yolks until very thick and lemon colored; stir into cottage cheese mixture. Stir about ¼ of the egg whites into cottage cheese mixture, then fold mixture into remaining egg whites.

Carefully pour into soufflé dish. Bake until knife inserted halfway between edge and center comes out clean, 50 to 60 minutes. Divide soufflé into sections with 2 forks.

FRIED TOMATOES

4 medium tomatoes (about 1½ pounds)
⅓ cup margarine
1 egg, beaten

1 cup dry bread crumbs
Salt and pepper

Cut thin slice from top and bottom of each tomato. Cut tomatoes into ¾-inch slices. Melt margarine in large skillet. Dip tomato slices into egg, then coat with bread crumbs. Cook in margarine, turning once, until golden brown, 3 to 4 minutes. Season with salt and pepper.   4 to 6 servings.

RELISH KABOBS

¼ green pepper, cut into 2×½-inch strips
1 stalk celery, cut into 2×1-inch pieces
4 radishes
1 carrot
¼ cucumber, cut into ¼-inch slices
4 stuffed olives (optional)

Insert a wooden pick in both ends of each green pepper strip to make a crescent shape. Make parallel cuts at both ends of each celery piece, cutting almost to center. Remove stems and root ends from radishes. Cut thin petals around radishes. With a vegetable parer, cut carrot into paper-thin strips. Roll up and fasten with wooden picks.

Place all vegetables except olives in bowl of ice and water; refrigerate about 3 hours. To serve, remove wooden picks from pepper strips and carrot curls; alternate vegetables on four 6-inch skewers or wooden picks.

TOASTED RYE BREAD WITH AVOCADO BUTTER

1 ripe avocado
2 teaspoons lemon juice
¼ to ½ teaspoon salt
⅛ teaspoon garlic salt
Dash pepper
4 slices toasted rye bread

Peel avocado; remove pit and cut avocado into pieces. Place all ingredients except rye bread in bowl. Mash with a fork until smooth. Cover and refrigerate until ready to serve. Spread on toasted rye bread.

PUMPKIN COOKIE-CAKE

1 envelope (about 2 ounces) dessert
  topping mix
¾ teaspoon cinnamon
¼ teaspoon nutmeg
⅛ teaspoon cloves
½ cup pumpkin
½ pound gingersnap cookies (30 cookies)

Prepare topping mix as directed on package. Stir in cinnamon, nutmeg, cloves and pumpkin. Spread about 2 teaspoons pumpkin mixture on each cookie; stack cookies together in groups of five (6 stacks). Arrange stacks two by two, close together on sides, in 2 rows on a piece of aluminum foil or waxed paper. Frost sides and tops with remaining pumpkin mixture. Refrigerate until cookies have softened, no longer than 4 hours. To serve, place cookie-cake on platter and cut diagonally.   4 to 6 servings.

POP ART...
FLUFFY DUMPLINGS
TOP A SHORT-CUT
GROUND BEEF STEW.

FOR FOUR
**Hamburger Medley
with Dumplings
Cucumbers Vinaigrette
Apples and Cheese Spread**

HAMBURGER MEDLEY WITH DUMPLINGS

1½ pounds ground beef	2 teaspoons salt
1 medium onion, chopped	½ teaspoon pepper
1 can (26 ounces) condensed vegetable beef soup	2¾ cups water
	Dumplings (below)
2 large potatoes, pared and diced	Parsley sprigs

Cook and stir meat and onion in Dutch oven until meat is brown and onion is tender. Stir in soup, potatoes, salt, pepper and water. Heat to boiling. Reduce heat; cover and simmer 20 minutes.

While meat and vegetables are simmering, prepare Dumplings except—do not stir in milk until ready to use. Drop dough by spoonfuls onto hot meat or potatoes (do not drop into liquid). Cook uncovered 10 minutes; keep simmering. Cover and cook until dumplings are fluffy, about 10 minutes. Garnish with parsley sprigs.

Dumplings

1½ cups all-purpose flour*	3 tablespoons shortening
2 teaspoons baking powder	¾ cup milk
¾ teaspoon salt	

Measure flour, baking powder and salt into bowl. Cut in shortening thoroughly, until mixture looks like meal. Stir in milk.

* If using self-rising flour, omit baking powder and salt.

CUCUMBERS VINAIGRETTE

1 medium cucumber	½ cup water
½ cup vinegar	½ teaspoon salt

Run tines of fork lengthwise on unpared cucumber. Slice cucumber thinly into shallow glass dish. Mix vinegar, water and salt; pour over cucumber. Cover and refrigerate at least 2 hours (no longer than 48 hours). Drain before serving.

IN THE CENTER: Herbed Pot Roast with
Vegetables (page 58).
CLOCKWISE, FROM ABOVE: Budget
Bouillabaisse (page 32), Midwestern Meat
Loaves (page 30), Smoky Corn Puffs (page 8),
Fish Stick Casserole (page 28), Crispy
Chicken (page 74).

IN THE CENTER: **Orange Blossom Salad Plate** (page 49).
CLOCKWISE, FROM ABOVE: Romaine Salad (page 11), **Best Beet Salad** (page 69), **Vegetable Marinade** (page 19), **Antipasto Vegetables** (page 13), **Peas 'n Carrot Salad** (page 14).

IN THE CENTER: *Zucchini-Tomato Combo* (page 28).
CLOCKWISE, FROM ABOVE: *Potato Pots with Peas 'n Carrots* (page 72), *Fried Tomatoes* (page 34), *Crunchy Sprouts* (page 74), *Stuffed Sweet Potatoes* (page 68).

IN THE CENTER: **Gingerbread with Orange Sauce** (page 15).
CLOCKWISE, FROM LEFT: **Melon Pie** (page 17),
Chocolate Puff Dessert (page 73), **Chocolate-Mint Roll** (page 45), **Rhubarb Cobbler** (page 47),
Meringue-frosted Cranberries (page 69),
Pumpkin Cookie-Cake (page 35).

SALMON GUMBO

1 can (16 ounces) okra, drained
1 clove garlic, minced
½ cup chopped onion
1 cup diced celery
½ cup chopped green pepper
2 tablespoons salad oil
¼ cup all-purpose flour
2 cups water
1 can (16 ounces) whole tomatoes

2 tablespoons lemon juice
½ teaspoon salt
1 bay leaf
½ teaspoon thyme leaves
¼ teaspoon paprika
⅛ teaspoon red pepper sauce
1 can (16 ounces) salmon
1½ cups hot cooked rice

In large skillet or Dutch oven, cook and stir okra, garlic, onion, celery and green pepper in oil until onion is tender, about 5 minutes. Stir in flour, then stir in water. Heat to boiling, stirring constantly. Boil and stir 1 minute. Add tomatoes, lemon juice, salt, bay leaf, thyme leaves, paprika and red pepper sauce. Heat to boiling, stirring constantly. Reduce heat; cover and simmer 20 minutes. Remove bay leaf.

Drain salmon; carefully remove bone and skin. Stir salmon into gumbo and heat through. Ladle gumbo into soup bowls; top with rice. Serve with additional red pepper sauce if desired.

Note: Serve with slices of French bread which have been spread with margarine, wrapped in foil and heated.

BAKED BANANAS ON CHOCOLATE ICE CREAM

3 green-tipped medium bananas
½ cup orange juice
2 tablespoons brown sugar

1½ teaspoons finely shredded orange peel
1 tablespoon margarine, softened
Chocolate ice cream

Heat oven to 375°. Peel bananas and cut each lengthwise in half; cut each half into 4 pieces. Place in ungreased shallow baking dish. Pour orange juice over bananas. Sprinkle brown sugar and orange peel on top; dot with margarine. Bake uncovered until bananas are tender, 15 to 20 minutes. Serve warm, on ice cream.

CREOLE...
A NEW-FASHIONED TWIST ON AN OLD NEW ORLEANS NUMBER.

FOR FIVE
Salmon Gumbo
Hot French Bread
Baked Bananas on
Chocolate Ice Cream

SAUCED ROUND STEAK

1 can (8 ounces) tomato sauce
½ teaspoon salt
2 tablespoons brown sugar
¼ teaspoon vinegar
¼ teaspoon Worcestershire sauce

¼ cup all-purpose flour
1½-pound beef round steak, ½ inch thick
Salt and pepper
1 medium onion, sliced
1 lemon, sliced

Fold a 60 × 18-inch piece of aluminum foil in half; place in jelly roll pan, 15½ × 10½ × 1 inch. Mix tomato sauce, ½ teaspoon salt, the brown sugar, vinegar, Worcestershire sauce and flour until smooth. Pour half the tomato mixture on center of foil in pan. Place meat on sauce. Season with salt and pepper; spread with remaining tomato mixture. Top with onion and lemon slices. Fold foil over meat and seal securely. Bake in 350° oven until tender, 1½ to 1¾ hours.

BAKED POTATOES

4 medium baking potatoes
(about 1½ pounds)

Margarine
¼ cup broken pretzel sticks

Heat oven to 350°. Scrub potatoes; if softer skins are desired, rub with shortening. Prick with a fork to allow steam to escape. Bake until soft, 1¼ to 1½ hours.

To serve, cut a crisscross gash in top of each; squeeze gently until some potato pops up through opening. Serve with margarine and top with pretzel pieces.

A GOOD-BUY WORD

One potato, two potato, three potato . . . packaged potato? Believe it or not, the last may be your best buy. Compare the going price of instant-type potatoes against that of produce-department potatoes on a per-serving basis. Then decide which way to go.

And don't discount their food value. A mere ½ cup of cooked potatoes constitutes one of the four "Fruit and Vegetable" servings everyone needs every day. "Too many calories," you say. Oh, no. There are only 80 calories in a medium potato. (It's what people put on the potato—butter, sour cream, whatever—that adds up.)

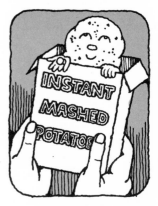

SCALLOPED CORN

2 tablespoons margarine
¼ cup chopped green onion
2 tablespoons flour
1 teaspoon salt
½ teaspoon paprika
¼ teaspoon dry mustard
Dash pepper

¾ cup milk
1 can (16 ounces) whole kernel corn, drained
1 egg, slightly beaten
⅓ cup cracker crumbs
1 tablespoon margarine, melted

Heat oven to 350°. Melt 2 tablespoons margarine in small saucepan. Add onion; cook and stir until tender. Remove from heat; stir in flour and seasonings. Cook over low heat, stirring constantly, until mixture is bubbly. Remove from heat; gradually stir in milk. Heat to boiling, stirring constantly. Boil and stir 1 minute. Stir in corn and egg. Pour into ungreased 1-quart casserole.

Mix cracker crumbs and 1 tablespoon margarine; sprinkle onto corn mixture. Bake uncovered 30 to 35 minutes.

JAM ROLL-UPS

6 slices white bread
½ package (3-ounce size) cream cheese, softened
1½ teaspoons jam

⅓ cup sugar
⅛ teaspoon nutmeg
¼ cup margarine, melted

Heat oven to 350°. Trim crusts from bread. Spread cream cheese on bread, then spread with jam. Cut each slice into 3 strips. Roll up each strip and secure with a wooden pick. Mix sugar and nutmeg. Dip rolls into margarine, then into sugar-nutmeg mixture. Place on ungreased baking sheet. Bake until crisp, 20 to 25 minutes.

TUNA BURGERS

1 can (9¾ ounces) tuna, drained
½ cup cracker crumbs
2 eggs, slightly beaten
1 tablespoon finely chopped green onion
1 teaspoon lemon juice
½ teaspoon salt

¼ teaspoon lemon pepper
¼ teaspoon chili powder
Dash hot sauce
Lettuce leaves
4 hamburger buns, split and toasted
2 tomatoes, sliced

Heat oven to 350°. Mix all ingredients except lettuce, buns and tomatoes. Press evenly in greased loaf pan, 8½ × 4½ × 2½ inches. Bake until firm and juicy, about 30 minutes. Cool in pan about 2 minutes, then remove from pan. Cut loaf into fourths; split each fourth horizontally in half. Place lettuce on each bun half; top with tuna and a tomato slice.   2 open-face burgers per serving.

CRISP-FRIED ONION RINGS

1 large Spanish or Bermuda onion
½ cup all-purpose flour*
2 tablespoons yellow cornmeal

¾ teaspoon baking powder
½ teaspoon salt
⅔ cup milk

Cut onion into ¼-inch slices and separate into rings. Soak rings in bowl of ice and water 30 minutes; drain and pat dry.

In large skillet or saucepan, heat 1 inch fat to 375°. Beat remaining ingredients with rotary beater until smooth. Dip onion rings into batter, allowing excess batter to drip into bowl. Fry a few rings at a time in hot fat, turning once, until golden brown, about 1½ minutes; drain. Sprinkle with salt.

* If using self-rising flour, omit baking powder and salt.

CREAMY LIME SALAD

1 can (8¼ ounces) crushed pineapple, drained (reserve syrup)
1 package (3 ounces) lime-flavored gelatin
1 package (3 ounces) cream cheese, softened
1 cup frozen whipped topping (thawed)
¼ cup chopped nuts

Add enough water to reserved pineapple syrup to measure 1½ cups. Heat to boiling. Pour boiling liquid onto gelatin in small mixer bowl; stir until gelatin is dissolved. Refrigerate until slightly thickened but not set.

Beat in cream cheese until gelatin is fluffy and cream cheese is broken into tiny pieces. Mix in pineapple, topping and nuts on low speed, scraping bowl occasionally. Pour into 3- or 4-cup mold. Refrigerate until firm, about 3 hours.

CHOCOLATE-MINT ROLL

¾ cup all-purpose flour *
¼ cup cocoa
1 teaspoon baking powder
¼ teaspoon salt
3 eggs
1 cup sugar
⅓ cup water
1 teaspoon vanilla
1 pint vanilla ice cream, softened
¼ cup crushed peppermint candy

Heat oven to 375°. Line jelly roll pan, 15½ × 10½ × 1 inch, with aluminum foil or waxed paper; grease. Mix flour, cocoa, baking powder and salt; set aside.

In small mixer bowl, beat eggs until very thick and lemon colored, about 5 minutes. Pour eggs into large mixer bowl; gradually beat in sugar. Mix in water and vanilla on low speed. Gradually beat in flour mixture until batter is smooth. Pour into pan, spreading batter to corners. Bake until a wooden pick inserted in center comes out clean, 12 to 15 minutes. Loosen cake from edges of pan; invert onto towel sprinkled with confectioners' sugar. Carefully remove foil; trim off stiff edges if necessary.

While hot, roll cake *and towel* from narrow end. Cool on wire rack. Unroll cake and remove towel. Spread ice cream on cake; sprinkle with crushed candy. Roll up; wrap in plastic wrap. Freeze until firm, about 6 hours. If you wish, sprinkle roll with additional confectioners' sugar. Cut half of roll into four 1-inch slices. Return remaining half of roll to freezer for another meal (within 2 weeks).   4 servings—and 4 for another meal.

* If using self-rising flour, omit baking powder and salt.

CHICKEN IN FOIL

⅓ cup all-purpose flour
2 teaspoons ginger
2½- to 3-pound broiler-fryer
  chicken, quartered
¼ cup margarine
1 package (10 ounces) frozen spinach,
  thawed

3 cups hot cooked rice
¼ cup finely chopped onion
2 teaspoons soy sauce
Salt and pepper
Curry Sauce (below)
¼ cup toasted coconut (see note)

Mix flour and ginger; coat chicken with flour mixture. Melt margarine in large skillet; brown chicken on both sides, 15 to 20 minutes.

Heat oven to 400°. On center of each of four 12-inch squares of heavy-duty aluminum foil, place ¼ of the spinach, ¼ of the rice, 1 tablespoon onion and a chicken quarter. Sprinkle each with ½ teaspoon soy sauce and season with salt and pepper. Fold foil over and seal securely. Place foil packages on ungreased baking sheet. Bake until chicken is tender, about 1 hour. To serve, remove from foil. Spoon Curry Sauce onto chicken and sprinkle with coconut.

Note: To toast coconut, heat oven to 350°; spread coconut in shallow baking pan and bake, stirring occasionally, until golden brown, 10 to 15 minutes.

Curry Sauce

2 tablespoons finely chopped onion
½ small clove garlic, finely chopped
1 tablespoon margarine
1 tablespoon flour

½ to ¾ teaspoon curry powder
¼ teaspoon ginger
1 cup milk

Cook and stir onion and garlic in margarine until onion is tender. Stir in flour, curry powder and ginger. Cook over low heat, stirring constantly, until mixture is bubbly. Remove from heat. Stir in milk. Heat to boiling, stirring constantly. Boil and stir 1 minute.

AVOCADO-PRUNE SALAD

1 avocado, cut into 12 slices
12 cooked prunes, cut into halves
Crisp salad greens
2 tablespoons salad oil

2 tablespoons orange juice
1 tablespoon lemon juice
1 tablespoon honey
½ teaspoon poppy seed

On each salad plate, arrange 3 avocado slices and 6 prune halves on salad greens. Shake remaining ingredients in tightly covered jar; drizzle about 2 tablespoons dressing onto each salad.

Variation

Pear-Prune Salad: Substitute 2 fresh pears, cut into 12 slices, or 1 can (8 ounces) sliced pears, drained, for the avocado.

RHUBARB COBBLER

3 cups cut-up rhubarb *
⅓ cup all-purpose flour
¼ cup brown sugar (packed)
½ cup granulated sugar

¼ teaspoon salt
1 cup buttermilk baking mix
¼ teaspoon almond extract
¼ cup water

Heat oven to 400°. Measure rhubarb into ungreased 1-quart casserole. Mix flour, sugars and salt; toss with rhubarb. Cover and bake 30 minutes.

Stir remaining ingredients until a soft dough forms. Remove casserole from oven; stir hot rhubarb to mix sauce and flour. Drop dough by spoonfuls (4) onto hot rhubarb. Bake uncovered until biscuit topping is golden brown, 20 to 25 minutes. Serve warm.

* You can substitute 1 can (16 ounces) rhubarb sauce for the fresh rhubarb. Omit flour, brown sugar, granulated sugar and salt.

A GOOD-BUY WORD

Everyone knows that whole chicken is one of the best bargains around. But few people capitalize on its full penny-wise potential. And all it takes is a bit of skillful knifework. Simply shop for good-size birds (the bigger the bird, the more meat to the pound), and cut them into parts yourself. Then check the comparable per-part purchases. Sneaky savings for the careful shopper! If you're lucky enough to have a freezer, be sure to take advantage of "specials" on chicken. Buy them in quantity and go to work with your knife. Sort the various parts and store them separately.

CURRIED BEEF

2 cups Coconut Milk (below)	⅓ cup finely chopped onion
1½ pounds beef stew meat	¼ teaspoon chili powder
1 teaspoon salt	½ teaspoon curry powder
2 tablespoons cider vinegar	Dash each cayenne red pepper and ginger
2 tablespoons salad oil	Snipped parsley
2 cloves garlic, finely chopped	3 to 4 cups hot cooked rice

Prepare Coconut Milk. Mix meat, salt and vinegar; let stand at room temperature no longer than 25 minutes, turning occasionally.

Heat oil in large skillet over medium heat. Remove meat from marinade. Brown meat in oil on all sides; remove meat. Cook and stir garlic and onion in same skillet (add 1 teaspoon oil if necessary) until onion is tender and golden brown, about 4 minutes. Stir in seasonings. Cook ½ minute. Add meat, turning to coat. Stir in Coconut Milk. Heat to boiling. Reduce heat; cover and simmer, stirring frequently, until meat is tender and glazed, about 1½ hours. Garnish with parsley; serve with rice.

Coconut Milk

Line small bowl with cheesecloth. Measure 2¼ cups flaked coconut into bowl. Pour 2 cups boiling water onto coconut; let stand at room temperature 20 minutes. Gather ends of cheesecloth together and squeeze liquid into the bowl—there should be 2 cups. Reserve coconut and use in Cream Coconut Dessert.

CUCUMBER-TOMATO YOGURT

1 medium cucumber	½ cup unflavored yogurt
1 green onion, finely chopped (with top)	¼ teaspoon salt
1 medium tomato, chopped	⅛ teaspoon ground cumin
1 teaspoon snipped parsley	

Pare cucumber and cut lengthwise in half. Scoop out seeds and cut cucumber into ½-inch pieces. Mix cucumber, onion, tomato and parsley; cover and refrigerate. Mix yogurt, salt and cumin; cover and refrigerate. At serving time, drain vegetables and fold into yogurt dressing.

BALI HA'I—CURRY, FRUIT AND COCONUT, EXOTIC TASTES IN A MINI-MONEY MENU.

FOR FOUR
Curried Beef
Cucumber-Tomato Yogurt
Orange Blossom Salad Plate
Cream Coconut Dessert

ORANGE BLOSSOM SALAD PLATE

1 large orange (see note)
1 tablespoon lemon juice
2 tablespoons honey

2 red apples
1 can (16 ounces) sliced peaches, drained (reserve syrup)

Squeeze juice from orange. Mix orange juice, lemon juice and honey; pour into small bowl and place on serving plate. Cut unpared apples into slices and dip into reserved peach syrup. Arrange apple and peach slices on serving plate.

Note: For a pretty, festive touch, cut 1-inch slice from top of orange, then squeeze juice from orange. Remove membranes from orange with a grapefruit spoon or melon-ball cutter, being careful not to break shell. Cut edge in a scalloped or saw-tooth design with a knife. Serve orange juice mixture in shell.

CREAM COCONUT DESSERT

2 cups reserved coconut (from Coconut Milk recipe at left)
3 tablespoons sugar
1 package (about 3½ ounces) vanilla pudding and pie filling

1 envelope (about 2 ounces) dessert topping mix
3 tablespoons margarine, melted
2 firm large bananas

Heat oven to 350°. Mix coconut and sugar; spread in ungreased shallow pan. Bake, stirring frequently, until coconut is golden brown, about 15 minutes. Turn into bowl and cool.

While coconut is baking, cook pudding and pie filling as directed on package for pudding; cool. Prepare topping mix as directed on package; set aside.

Mix baked coconut and margarine (if desired, reserve 2 tablespoons of this mixture for garnish). Pat coconut mixture in bottom of ungreased baking pan, 8×8×2 inches. Slice 1 banana and spread slices evenly over coconut mixture. Pour ¾ cup of the pudding over slices. Slice remaining banana and spread slices evenly on pudding. Top with remaining pudding and the topping. Garnish with reserved coconut mixture. Refrigerate at least 4 hours. Cut into 9 squares.

AUTUMN STEW

¼ cup all-purpose flour
1½ teaspoons salt
¼ teaspoon paprika
¼ teaspoon pepper
1½ pounds beef stew meat,
    cut into 1-inch pieces
2 tablespoons shortening
1 can (16 ounces) stewed tomatoes
2 cups water

½ cup chopped onion
1 clove garlic, finely chopped
2 beef bouillon cubes
1 teaspoon pumpkin pie spice
3 medium potatoes, pared and cut into
    1-inch cubes
2½ cups 1-inch cubes pumpkin or
    Hubbard squash

Mix flour, salt, paprika and pepper; coat meat with flour mixture. Melt shortening in Dutch oven; brown meat. Stir in remaining ingredients except potatoes and pumpkin. Heat to boiling. Reduce heat; cover and simmer until meat is almost tender, about 2 hours. Stir in potatoes and pumpkin; cover and simmer until vegetables are tender, about 30 minutes.

CELERY STICKS AND APPLE WEDGES

Cut 2 stalks celery into sticks. Cut 2 apples into wedges and remove cores. Arrange on plates.

TART LEMON PUDDING

2 cups sugar
½ cup cornstarch
2 cups water
4 egg yolks, slightly beaten

¼ cup margarine
2 teaspoons grated lemon peel
⅔ cup lemon juice

Mix sugar and cornstarch in 2-quart saucepan; gradually stir in water. Cook over medium heat, stirring constantly, until mixture thickens and boils. Boil and stir 1 minute.

Gradually stir at least half the hot mixture into egg yolks. Stir egg yolk mixture into hot mixture in saucepan. Heat to boiling, stirring constantly. Boil and stir 2 minutes.

Remove from heat; stir in margarine, lemon peel and lemon juice. Pour into 4 dessert dishes and refrigerate.

3

Well-Planned Splurges

BROILED HALIBUT

1 **package (16 ounces) frozen halibut fillets, thawed**	½ **teaspoon salt**
2 **tablespoons margarine, melted**	¼ **teaspoon paprika**
½ **teaspoon vinegar**	1 **tablespoon thinly sliced green onion**

If fillets are large, cut into serving pieces; place on rack in broiler pan. Mix remaining ingredients except onion; brush part of mixture on top of fish.

Set oven control at broil and/or 550°. Broil fish with top 3 to 4 inches from heat until golden brown, 6 to 7 minutes. Turn fish carefully; brush with remaining mixture. Broil until fish flakes easily with a fork, 6 to 7 minutes longer. Place fish on warm serving platter; sprinkle with green onion.

LEMON MASHED POTATOES

Prepare instant mashed potato puffs as directed on package for 4 servings except—stir in 1 teaspoon grated lemon peel and 2 teaspoons lemon juice.

PEAS-TOMATO TARRAGON

1 **package (10 ounces) frozen green peas**	1 **tablespoon margarine**
1 **tomato, cut into 8 wedges**	¼ **teaspoon tarragon leaves**

Cook peas as directed on package except—add tomato wedges for the last 2 minutes of cooking; drain. Toss peas, tomato wedges, margarine and tarragon leaves.

CREAMY PEAR COLESLAW

3 **cups shredded cabbage (about ½ medium)**	2 **tablespoons orange juice**
2 **pears, diced***	½ **teaspoon salt**
⅓ **cup mandarin orange yogurt**	⅛ **to ¼ teaspoon nutmeg**
¼ **cup salad dressing**	**Finely shredded orange peel**

Toss cabbage and pears in large bowl. Mix remaining ingredients except orange peel; toss with cabbage and pears. Garnish with orange peel.

You can substitute 1 can (8 ounces) sliced pears, drained and diced, for the fresh pears.

One turkey breast, about 5 pounds, is the starting point for two delicious—and different—turkey dinners.

Remove bones from turkey breast, cutting close to bones and being careful to leave skin in one piece. Cut meat in a single piece from one half. Use this piece for the Baked Turkey Breast.

Sprinkle 1 teaspoon seasoned salt and ½ teaspoon lemon pepper on the breast half with skin. (This piece can be used later for the Soy-Honey Turkey Breast.) Roll up from narrow end; wrap in skin and secure with skewers. Wrap in aluminum foil and freeze (no longer than 1 month). Serve at another meal with remaining menu suggestions.

BAKED TURKEY BREAST

2½-pound turkey breast half
1 can (2 ounces) mushroom stems and
  pieces, drained
¼ cup dry bread crumbs
¼ cup snipped parsley
2 tablespoons soft margarine
1 teaspoon tarragon leaves
½ teaspoon salt

¼ teaspoon pepper
¼ cup plus 2 tablespoons margarine,
  melted
1 chicken bouillon cube
¾ cup water
2 tablespoons margarine
1 tablespoon flour

Heat oven to 400°. Place turkey breast half boned side down and pound into oblong, 13 × 8 inches. Mix mushrooms, bread crumbs, parsley, 2 tablespoons soft margarine, the tarragon leaves, salt and pepper. Spread on turkey breast. Roll up from narrow end; wrap in aluminum foil and place in ungreased baking pan. Bake 30 minutes; open foil. Bake turkey breast 25 minutes, basting frequently with melted margarine. Increase oven temperature to 500°; bake just until brown, about 5 minutes. Remove turkey to warm serving plate.

Pour drippings into small saucepan. Stir in bouillon cube, water, 2 tablespoons margarine and the flour. Heat to boiling, stirring constantly. Boil and stir 1 minute. Season with salt and pepper. Serve with turkey.

2-TIMER...
DO A DOUBLE-TAKE
TREATMENT ON THIS
ONE-TURKEY BUY.

FOR FIVE
**Baked Turkey Breast
or Soy-Honey Turkey
Breast
Panfried Spinach
Honeyed Melon Salad
Corn Biscuit Sticks
Parfaits au Chocolat**

SOY-HONEY TURKEY BREAST

2½-pound frozen rolled turkey breast
1 beef bouillon cube
½ cup boiling water
3 tablespoons honey
3 tablespoons soy sauce

1 tablespoon vinegar
1 clove garlic, finely chopped
1 teaspoon ginger
2 tablespoons flour
Salt and pepper

Heat oven to 325°. Remove frozen rolled turkey breast from foil wrapping; place on rack in shallow roasting pan. Roast uncovered 1 hour. Remove skewers and insert meat thermometer; roast until thermometer registers 130°, about 45 minutes.

Dissolve bouillon cube in boiling water. Mix in honey, soy sauce, vinegar, garlic and ginger. Roast, basting turkey frequently with soy-honey mixture, until thermometer registers 170°, about 1½ hours. Remove turkey to warm serving plate.

Skim fat from drippings; reserve 2 tablespoons fat in small saucepan. Mix in flour. Cook over low heat, stirring constantly, until mixture is smooth and bubbly. Remove from heat. Strain drippings into measuring cup; add enough water to measure 1 cup. Stir into flour mixture. Heat to boiling, stirring constantly. Boil and stir 1 minute. Season with salt and pepper. Serve with turkey.

PANFRIED SPINACH

2 slices bacon
1 clove garlic, crushed
2 packages (10 ounces each) frozen
  leaf spinach, thawed

Salt and pepper
Vinegar

Fry bacon until crisp; remove and drain bacon. Cook garlic in bacon fat remaining in skillet until tender. Press water from spinach. Cook and stir spinach in bacon fat until wilted, about 1 minute. Cover skillet 30 seconds. Season with salt and pepper; crumble bacon on spinach. Serve with vinegar.

HONEYED MELON SALAD

3 cups watermelon balls (about ¼ watermelon)

2 cups cantaloupe balls (1 cantaloupe)
2 tablespoons honey

Toss melon balls and honey in serving dish. Refrigerate until ready to serve.

Note: If melons are not in season, serve Spicy Peach Salad (page 70) instead.

CORN BISCUIT STICKS

1 tablespoon yellow cornmeal
¾ cup buttermilk baking mix
¼ cup cornmeal

¼ cup milk
1 tablespoon soft margarine
½ to 1 teaspoon salt

Heat oven to 450°. Sprinkle 1 tablespoon cornmeal on greased baking sheet. Mix baking mix, ¼ cup cornmeal and the milk until a soft dough forms. Pat dough on baking sheet into rectangle, 10×4 inches. Bake until golden brown, about 10 minutes. Brush with margarine; sprinkle with salt. Cut crosswise into 1-inch sticks.   10 sticks.

PARFAITS AU CHOCOLAT

1 package (about 3 ounces) vanilla pudding and pie filling
1⅓ cups water

⅔ cup nonfat dry milk
5 tablespoons chocolate ice-cream topping
1 cup frozen whipped topping (thawed)

Mix pudding and pie filling, water and dry milk in saucepan. Cook over medium heat, stirring constantly, just to boiling. Remove from heat; cool.

Layer pudding, chocolate topping and whipped topping in 5 parfait glasses. Garnish with maraschino cherries for added color.

A GOOD-BUY WORD

When it comes to those holiday crowd-fests, go for the big birds every time—you'll get more for your money. You can follow the same budget-beating route for regular family fare. Simply store the leftovers —in the refrigerator if you plan to use them soon (within 2 days) or in the freezer if your plans are more long range (within 6 months for turkey stored with broth or gravy, within 1 month for plain turkey).

DANDY!
A YANKEE-DOODLE
DEAL FEATURING
ALL-TIME FAVORITES.

FOR SIX
**Herbed Pot Roast
with Vegetables
Potato Rolls
Blueberry Special**

HERBED POT ROAST WITH VEGETABLES

4-pound beef chuck pot roast (arm, blade, boneless chuck eye, cross rib, boneless shoulder)
1 teaspoon salt
¼ teaspoon pepper
½ teaspoon marjoram leaves
¼ teaspoon basil leaves
2 cloves garlic, crushed

¼ cup apple cider
¼ cup water
5 medium carrots, cut into 2-inch pieces
4 medium white turnips, quartered
1 medium onion, quartered
1 cup 1-inch pieces celery
1 green pepper, cut into 1-inch pieces
2 tablespoons snipped parsley

Trim excess fat from meat. Grease Dutch oven with fat; brown meat over medium heat, about 10 minutes. Sprinkle salt, pepper, marjoram leaves, basil leaves and garlic onto meat; add cider and water. Heat to boiling. Reduce heat; cover and simmer 1½ hours. Add vegetables and parsley. If necessary, pour in ¼ cup water. Cover and simmer until vegetables and meat are tender, about 35 minutes.

POTATO ROLLS

1 package active dry yeast
1½ cups warm water (105 to 115°)
⅔ cup sugar
1½ teaspoons salt

⅔ cup shortening
2 eggs
1 cup lukewarm mashed potatoes
7 to 7½ cups all-purpose flour*

In large bowl, dissolve yeast in warm water. Stir in sugar, salt, shortening, eggs, potatoes and 4 cups of the flour. Beat until smooth. Mix in enough remaining flour to make dough easy to handle.

Turn dough onto lightly floured board; knead until smooth and elastic, about 5 minutes. Place in greased bowl; turn greased side up. Cover bowl tightly; refrigerate at least 8 hours or until ready to use. (Dough can be kept up to 5 days in refrigerator at 45° or below. Keep covered.)

Punch down dough; prepare one of the variations at right. Let rise in warm place 1½ hours before baking. Heat oven to 400°. Bake rolls 15 to 25 minutes. (Use remaining dough in another variation.)

* If using self-rising flour, omit salt.

Variations

Casserole Rolls: Using ¼ of the dough, shape bits into 1-inch balls. Place in lightly greased layer pan, 9×1½ inches. Brush with soft margarine.　　36 rolls.

Cloverleaf Rolls: Using ¼ of the dough, shape bits into 1-inch balls. Place 3 balls in each greased muffin cup. Brush with soft margarine.　　12 rolls.

Pan Biscuits: Using half the dough, roll on lightly floured board into rectangle, 13×9 inches. Place in greased baking pan, 13×9×2 inches. Score dough ¼ inch deep into 15 rolls. Brush with soft margarine.　　15 rolls.

BLUEBERRY SPECIAL

1 cup boiling water
1 package (3 ounces) lemon-flavored gelatin
1 package (3 ounces) black cherry-flavored gelatin
1 cup cold water
1 tablespoon lemon juice
1 can (21 ounces) blueberry pie filling
1 cup unflavored yogurt
¼ cup confectioners' sugar

Pour boiling water onto gelatin in bowl; stir until gelatin is dissolved. Stir in cold water, lemon juice and pie filling. Pour into baking pan, 8×8×2 inches. Cover and refrigerate until firm.

Cut into 9 squares. Mix yogurt and confectioners' sugar; serve on squares.

A GOOD-BUY WORD

The number one rule for meat-buying: Forget about the price per pound, it's the price per serving that counts in the cashbox. Here are general guidelines:
 • Boneless meat—4 servings per pound
 • Meat with bone—2 to 3 servings per pound
 • Meat with a large bone—1 to 2 servings per pound

COOL IT–
THE PERFECT
PLAN FOR A SULTRY
SUMMER EVENING.

FOR FOUR
Frosted Fruit Cooler
Tuna Salad Niçoise
Cheese Sticks
Strawberry Cream
Shortcake

FROSTED FRUIT COOLER

1 cup water
¼ cup sugar
2 cups chilled fruit juice*
2 tablespoons lemon juice

Red food color (optional)
Sherbet
4 lemon slices

Heat water and sugar to boiling. Reduce heat; simmer uncovered 20 minutes. Cover and refrigerate.

Mix fruit juice and lemon juice into sugar syrup. Stir in a few drops of food color. Pour into 4 small glasses. Top each with a scoop of sherbet and garnish with a lemon slice.

Use your favorite juice or try any combination of fresh or canned fruit juices or the syrup drained from canned fruits or fresh fruit sauces.

TUNA SALAD NICOISE

3 cups bite-size pieces salad greens
2 cups diced cooked potato, chilled
1 can (16 ounces) French-style green
  beans, drained and chopped
2 cans (6½ ounces each) tuna, drained
2 hard-cooked eggs, cut into wedges
2 tomatoes, cut into 16 wedges

12 pimiento-stuffed green olives
¼ cup salad oil
¼ cup vinegar
1 small clove garlic, finely chopped
½ teaspoon salt
¼ teaspoon pepper

Divide salad greens among 4 large salad plates or individual salad bowls. Mix potato and green beans. For each serving, spoon about ¼ of the potato-bean mixture into 1-cup measuring cup or custard cup. Press down firmly (the cup should be about ¾ full); unmold onto center of salad greens.

Arrange tuna, egg and tomato wedges around potato-bean molds; garnish with olives. Shake remaining ingredients in tightly covered jar; pour over salads.

CHEESE STICKS

1 cup shredded pasteurized process cheese
  spread loaf
1 tablespoon flour
1 teaspoon prepared mustard

1 tablespoon finely chopped onion
1 tablespoon snipped parsley
⅛ teaspoon red pepper sauce
4 slices bread

Set oven control at broil and/or 550°. Mix all ingredients except bread. Place bread on ungreased baking sheet. Broil about 6 inches from heat until golden brown, about 1½ minutes; turn. Spread cheese mixture evenly on bread. Broil until cheese is melted and bubbly, 1½ to 2 minutes. Cut each slice of bread into 3 sticks.   12 sticks.

STRAWBERRY CREAM SHORTCAKE

1 package (about 3 ounces) vanilla
  pudding and pie filling
3 eggs
1 cup sugar
⅓ cup water
1 teaspoon vanilla

¾ cup all-purpose flour
1 teaspoon baking powder
¼ teaspoon salt
¼ cup flaked coconut
1 package (10 ounces) frozen strawberry
  halves, slightly thawed

Cook pudding and pie filling as directed except—decrease milk to 1½ cups.

Heat oven to 350°. Grease and flour baking pan, 9×9×2 inches. In small mixer bowl, beat eggs until very thick and lemon colored, about 5 minutes. Pour eggs into large mixer bowl; gradually beat in sugar. Mix in water and vanilla on low speed. Gradually add flour, baking powder and salt, beating just until batter is smooth. Pour into pan, spreading batter to corners.

Bake until wooden pick inserted in center comes out clean, 25 to 30 minutes. Loosen cake from edges of pan and remove from pan. Cool on wire rack.

Split cake horizontally into 2 layers. Fill layers with ¾ cup vanilla filling. Spread remaining filling on top; sprinkle with coconut. Refrigerate at least 2 hours.

Cut 4 servings from half the cake and top each with strawberries. Refrigerate remaining cake and serve the next day with a different topping (store no longer than 24 hours).   4 servings—and 4 for another meal.

Note: Any fresh fruit or drained canned fruit can be used as a topping for this cake.

MARINATED BEEF TIP

5-pound beef tip roast
1½ cups apple cider
¼ cup salad oil
3 tablespoons cider vinegar
1 tablespoon chopped green onion
1 clove garlic, crushed
1 bay leaf

½ teaspoon salt
¼ teaspoon thyme
Dash pepper
3 slices bacon
1 beef bouillon cube
1 cup boiling water

Place meat in plastic bag. Shake cider, oil, vinegar, onion, garlic, bay leaf, salt, thyme and pepper in tightly covered jar. Pour over meat in bag. Place bag in bowl or shallow dish; refrigerate at least 12 hours.

Fry bacon in Dutch oven until crisp; remove and drain bacon. Remove meat from marinade; reserve ½ cup marinade. Brown roast in bacon fat remaining in Dutch oven over medium heat about 20 minutes. Crumble bacon on meat. Dissolve bouillon cube in boiling water; pour reserved marinade and the bouillon into Dutch oven. Insert meat thermometer so tip is in thickest part of meat. Cover and cook in 325° oven until meat thermometer registers 160°, 2 to 2½ hours. Remove meat to warm platter; let stand 10 to 15 minutes before slicing. If desired, make gravy from liquid remaining in pan.   6 servings—and 6 servings for another meal (see Beef Orientale, page 64).

PARSLEYED POTATOES AND CARROTS

5 medium potatoes (about 2 pounds), pared
4 medium carrots

¼ cup margarine, melted
1 tablespoon snipped parsley

Cut potatoes and carrots into large pieces. Heat 1 inch salted water (½ teaspoon salt to 1 cup water) to boiling in large saucepan. Add potatoes and carrots; cover and heat to boiling. Reduce heat; simmer until tender, 30 to 35 minutes. Drain. Pour margarine onto vegetables and sprinkle with parsley; toss.

TIP TOP!
TENDER TREATMENT
AND ELEGANT ASIDES
MAKE THE MOST (FOR
THE LEAST) OF THIS
ROAST BEEF REPAST.

FOR SIX
Marinated Beef Tip
Parsleyed Potatoes
and Carrots
Two-Apple Salad
Baked Cup Custard

TWO-APPLE SALAD

1 jar (14 ounces) spiced apple slices, chilled
3 medium apples, cut into thin wedges
Crisp salad greens

½ cup finely chopped celery
¼ cup salad dressing or mayonnaise

Cut each spiced apple slice in half. On each salad plate, arrange the half-slices and thin apple wedges on greens; sprinkle with celery. Serve with salad dressing.

BAKED CUP CUSTARD

3 eggs, slightly beaten
⅓ cup sugar
Dash salt

1 teaspoon vanilla
2½ cups milk, scalded
Nutmeg

Heat oven to 350°. Mix eggs, sugar, salt and vanilla. Gradually stir in milk. Pour into six 6-ounce custard cups. Sprinkle with nutmeg. Place cups in baking pan, 13×9×2 inches; pour very hot water into pan to within ½ inch of tops of cups.

Bake until knife inserted halfway between center and edge comes out clean, about 45 minutes. Remove cups from water; let stand at room temperature 10 minutes. Refrigerate.

A GOOD-BUY WORD

Protein-packed eggs have some sizable differences, ranging from extra large to large to medium to small. Be sure to check the prices carefully—if, within the same grade, there is *less than* a 7-cent difference per dozen between one size and the next larger size, then by all means go for the biggies. More than 7 cents? They're not worth it.

CHOW'S ON! THE TASTES OF THE ORIENT TURN A NEW LEAF ON THE LEFTOVER.

FOR SIX
Beef Orientale
Ginger Beet Salad
Empress Pie

BEEF ORIENTALE

Leftover cooked beef tip roast
  (from Marinated Beef Tip, page 62)
3 tablespoons margarine
1 can (20 ounces) pineapple chunks,
  drained (reserve syrup)
1 tablespoon vinegar
2 tablespoons soy sauce
1 tablespoon Worcestershire sauce
1 tablespoon sugar

¼ teaspoon salt
2 tablespoons cornstarch
2 tablespoons water
1 medium green pepper, cut into 1-inch
  pieces
1 medium tomato, cut into sixths
1 medium onion, thinly sliced
1 package (8 ounces) chow mein noodles

Cut meat into 1-inch pieces (about 6 cups). Melt margarine in 10-inch skillet; brown meat over medium-high heat, about 5 minutes. Add enough water to reserved pineapple syrup to measure 2¼ cups. Stir pineapple liquid, vinegar, soy sauce, Worcestershire sauce, sugar and salt into skillet; simmer 4 minutes. Mix cornstarch and water; gradually stir into meat mixture. Cook, stirring constantly, until mixture thickens and boils. Stir in pineapple chunks and vegetables; cook until glazed and hot, about 2 minutes. Serve on chow mein noodles.

GINGER BEET SALAD

1 can (16 ounces) sliced beets, chilled
  and drained
2 medium oranges, pared and sliced

Crisp lettuce leaves
Ginger Dressing (below)
Snipped parsley

On each salad plate, arrange beets and orange slices on lettuce leaves. Drizzle dressing onto salads; sprinkle with parsley.

Ginger Dressing

3 tablespoons salad oil
½ teaspoon vinegar
¼ teaspoon lemon juice

¼ teaspoon ginger
¼ teaspoon salt

Shake all ingredients in tightly covered jar.

EMPRESS PIE

Peanut-Graham Cracker Crust (below)
¼ cup margarine
¼ cup confectioners' sugar
2 eggs, separated
½ teaspoon vanilla
1 ounce melted unsweetened chocolate
(cool)

¼ teaspoon cream of tartar
½ cup confectioners' sugar
1 envelope (about 2 ounces) dessert
topping mix
1 large banana
Maraschino cherries

Prepare crust. Mix margarine and ¼ cup confectioners' sugar. Beat in egg yolks, vanilla and chocolate until mixture is creamy and fluffy. Beat egg whites and cream of tartar until foamy. Beat in ½ cup confectioners' sugar, 1 tablespoon at a time; beat until stiff and glossy (do not underbeat). Fold chocolate mixture into egg white meringue.

Prepare dessert topping mix as directed on package. Reserve ½ cup dessert topping for garnish. Fold chocolate mixture into remaining dessert topping.

Slice banana into crust; arrange slices in single layer. Turn chocolate mixture into crust; spread evenly. Refrigerate pie until set, about 4 hours. Garnish with reserved dessert topping and the cherries.

Peanut-Graham Cracker Crust

1¼ cups graham cracker crumbs
(about 16 crackers)
2 tablespoons sugar

¼ cup margarine, melted
¼ cup chopped Spanish peanuts

Heat oven to 350°. Mix all ingredients. Press mixture firmly and evenly against bottom and side of 9-inch pie pan. Bake 10 minutes; cool.

A GOOD-BUY WORD

Is the milk bill milking your budget? You can cut down on costs without cutting down on your daily intake. (Most people need at least 2 cups a day.) Instead of fluid milk, use reconstituted nonfat dry milk. Start off with a blend of the two, then gradually reduce the proportion of fluid milk. No one will be the wiser. And when it comes to cooking, look to evaporated milk: Equal parts of water and evaporated milk do the job of whole milk.

PLUM-BARBECUED SPARERIBS

4 pounds spareribs, cut into serving
  pieces
1 tablespoon salt
1 can (16 ounces) whole purple plums,
  drained (reserve syrup)
1 tablespoon brown sugar

3 tablespoons chopped onion
2 teaspoons soy sauce
¼ teaspoon grated lemon peel
¼ teaspoon cinnamon
Dash cloves and nutmeg
3 drops red food color

Place spareribs in Dutch oven. Add enough water to cover spareribs (about 3 quarts) and the salt. Heat to boiling. Reduce heat; cover and simmer 40 minutes. Drain.

While spareribs are cooking, remove pits from plums. Sieve plums into medium saucepan. Stir reserved plum syrup and remaining ingredients into plum pulp. Heat to boiling, stirring constantly. Cook 3 minutes, stirring constantly.

Arrange spareribs meaty side up on rack in shallow roasting pan. Spread with ⅔ cup of the plum sauce. Roast uncovered in 375° oven until tender and glazed, about 45 minutes, basting with remaining plum sauce 3 times during the roasting period.

BUTTERED BROCCOLI

⅓ package (20-ounce size) frozen
  chopped broccoli

2 tablespoons margarine

Cook broccoli as directed on package. Dot with margarine; toss.

CONFETTI COTTAGE CHEESE

2 cups creamed cottage cheese
  (small curd)
1 green onion, thinly sliced
⅓ cup thinly sliced celery

⅛ teaspoon salt
Dash pepper
Crisp salad greens
Radish slices or snipped parsley

Mix cottage cheese, onion, celery, salt and pepper. Cover and refrigerate at least 1 hour (no longer than 24 hours). Serve on salad greens; garnish with radish slices.

LEMON MUFFINS

1 egg
2 tablespoons salad oil
½ cup buttermilk
1 cup all-purpose flour

2 tablespoons sugar
1½ teaspoons baking powder
½ teaspoon salt
½ teaspoon grated lemon peel

Heat oven to 375°. Grease bottoms of 6 medium muffin cups or use paper baking cups. Beat egg, oil and buttermilk in medium bowl. Stir in remaining ingredients just until flour is moistened. Batter should be lumpy. Fill muffin cups ⅔ full. Bake until golden brown, 20 to 25 minutes. Remove muffins from pan immediately.   6 muffins.

PRUNE PUDDING

1 cup cooked pitted prunes
¾ cup oatmeal*
¼ teaspoon cinnamon
¼ teaspoon salt

¼ teaspoon lemon juice
2 egg whites
¼ cup sugar

Mash prunes in medium bowl; stir in oatmeal, cinnamon, salt and lemon juice. Beat egg whites until foamy. Beat in sugar, 1 tablespoon at a time; beat until stiff and glossy (do not underbeat). Fold prune mixture into egg white meringue. Turn into 1-quart serving dish. Refrigerate until set.

* Use leftover oatmeal or prepare ¾ cup as directed on package.

ROCK CORNISH HENS

3 **Rock Cornish hens (about 1¼ pounds each)**
10 **slices dried beef**
½ **cup margarine**
½ **cup chopped onion**
¾ **cup chopped celery (stalks and leaves)**

¼ **teaspoon finely chopped garlic**
2 **tablespoons snipped parsley**
½ **teaspoon poultry seasoning**
¼ **teaspoon pepper**
1¾ **cups soft bread cubes**
Melted margarine

Thaw hens if frozen. Snip dried beef into small pieces. Melt ½ cup margarine in large skillet. Add dried beef, onion, celery and garlic; cook and stir until onion and celery are tender, about 6 minutes. Remove from heat; stir in parsley, poultry seasoning, pepper and bread cubes and toss.

Heat oven to 350°. Stuff each hen with about 6 tablespoons stuffing. Secure opening with skewers. Fasten neck skin to back. Place hens breast side up on rack in shallow roasting pan. Brush with melted margarine. Roast hens uncovered until tender and golden brown, about 1 hour, brushing with margarine 5 or 6 times during the roasting period.

To serve, cut hens in half with kitchen scissors, cutting along backbone from tail to neck.

STUFFED SWEET POTATOES

6 **medium sweet potatoes**
⅓ **cup milk**
3 **tablespoons margarine**

¾ **teaspoon salt**
⅛ **teaspoon pepper**
Nutmeg

Heat oven to 350°. Prick sweet potatoes with a fork. Bake until tender, about 1¼ hours.

Increase oven temperature to 400°. Cut thin slice from top of each potato; scoop out insides, leaving thin shells of potato. Mash scooped-out potato until no lumps remain. Add milk, margarine, salt and pepper; beat vigorously until light and fluffy. Fill potato shells with mashed potato mixture and sprinkle with nutmeg. Bake on ungreased baking sheet 20 minutes.

BEST BEET SALAD

1 large head lettuce, torn into bite-size pieces
3 green onions, chopped (with tops)

1 jar (16 ounces) pickled sliced beets, drained
Budget Blue Cheese Dressing (below)

Layer ¼ each lettuce pieces, green onions and beets in large bowl; repeat 3 times. Serve with Budget Blue Cheese Dressing.

Budget Blue Cheese Dressing

⅔ cup mayonnaise or salad dressing
¼ cup nonfat dry milk
3 tablespoons pasteurized blue cheese spread
2 tablespoons water

½ teaspoon Worcestershire sauce
¼ teaspoon garlic salt
¼ teaspoon lemon juice
Dash pepper
Dash red pepper sauce

In small mixer bowl, beat all ingredients until smooth. Refrigerate 3 hours in tightly covered jar.

MERINGUE-FROSTED CRANBERRIES

1½ cups water
1¼ cups sugar
1 pound cranberries
2 tablespoons strawberry preserves
2 egg whites

⅛ teaspoon cream of tartar
¼ cup sugar
¼ teaspoon vanilla
About ¼ cup plus 2 tablespoons coconut

Heat water and 1¼ cups sugar in 3-quart saucepan, stirring until sugar is dissolved. Heat to boiling; boil 5 minutes. Stir in cranberries. Heat to boiling; boil until thickened, 5 to 7 minutes. Stir in strawberry preserves. Divide among six ½-cup custard cups.

Heat oven to 400°. Beat egg whites and cream of tartar until foamy. Beat in ¼ cup sugar, 1 tablespoon at a time; beat until stiff and glossy (do not underbeat). Stir in vanilla.

Sprinkle about 1 tablespoon coconut onto fruit mixture in each custard cup. Heap egg white meringue onto coconut. Bake until golden brown, about 10 minutes. Cool slightly (away from draft). Serve warm.

CHINA FRY— A DEEP BOW TO THE EAST, FROM FIRST COURSE TO LAST.

FOR FOUR
Chinese Pork and Vegetables
Hot Rice
Spicy Peach Salad
Fortune Cookies
Sherbet

CHINESE PORK AND VEGETABLES

1½ pounds pork blade or arm steak
1 tablespoon salad oil
1 chicken bouillon cube
1½ cups boiling water
⅓ cup chopped onion
⅓ cup coarsely chopped green pepper
1 can (4 ounces) mushroom stems and pieces, drained

2 tablespoons salad oil
1 can (16 ounces) chow mein vegetables, drained
3 tablespoons soy sauce
2 tablespoons cornstarch
¼ cup water
4 cups hot cooked rice

Trim excess fat from meat; cut meat into ¼- to ½-inch cubes. Heat 1 tablespoon oil in large skillet; brown meat. Drain off fat. Dissolve bouillon cube in boiling water; pour ⅓ cup of the bouillon on meat. Cover and simmer until tender, about 25 minutes. Remove meat and liquid from skillet; set aside.

In same skillet, cook and stir onion, green pepper and mushrooms in 2 tablespoons oil until crisp-tender, about 5 minutes. Stir in meat and liquid, chow mein vegetables, remaining bouillon and the soy sauce. Mix cornstarch and ¼ cup water; gradually stir into meat mixture. Cook, stirring constantly, until mixture thickens and boils. Boil and stir 1 minute. Serve on rice.

SPICY PEACH SALAD

1 can (16 ounces) peach halves, drained (reserve ¼ cup syrup)
½ cup water
1 tablespoon lemon juice
1 cinnamon stick, broken into 1-inch pieces

4 whole cloves
⅛ teaspoon ginger
1 can (14½ ounces) pineapple slices, drained
Crisp salad greens
Strawberry or raspberry preserves or jam

Heat peaches, reserved peach syrup, the water, lemon juice, cinnamon stick, cloves and ginger in saucepan, stirring gently, until mixture boils. Reduce heat; simmer 10 minutes. Spoon peaches and spices into pint jar. Pour hot syrup over peaches. Cover and refrigerate at least 4 hours (no longer than 4 days).

Arrange pineapple slices on salad greens. Place peach half cut side up on each pineapple slice and spoon about ½ teaspoon preserves into center.

FORTUNE COOKIES

2½ dozen paper fortunes (2½ × ½ inch)
½ cup all-purpose flour
¼ cup sugar
1 tablespoon cornstarch

Dash salt
1 teaspoon almond extract
2 egg whites
¼ cup salad oil

Prepare paper fortunes. Heat oven to 300°. Mix flour, sugar, cornstarch and salt. Add almond extract, egg whites and oil; beat until smooth.

Generously grease baking sheet. Bake only 4 cookies at a time. (Cool sheet after each baking and grease generously each time.) For each cookie, spoon 1 heaping teaspoonful batter onto baking sheet; with back of spoon, spread into 3½-inch circle. Bake until golden brown, about 10 minutes.

Working quickly, remove 1 cookie at a time with wide spatula; flip into protected hand. (Leave remaining cookies in oven.) Place paper fortune on center of cookie and fold cookie in half. Holding points of folded cookie with both hands, place center of fold over edge of bowl and pull points downward to make a crease across center. Place cookie in ungreased muffin cup so it will hold its shape while cooling. If cookie cools before it is formed, heat in oven about 1 minute. Store cookies in tightly covered container.   About 2 dozen cookies.

CHERRY-GLAZED LAMB

¼ cup all-purpose flour
2 teaspoons salt
¼ teaspoon pepper
4 lamb shanks (¾ pound each)

⅓ cup shortening
¾ cup water
Cherry Glaze (below)

Mix flour, salt and pepper; coat meat with flour mixture. Melt shortening in Dutch oven; brown meat over medium-high heat. Drain off fat. Pour water into Dutch oven. Cover and bake in 325° oven 1 hour.

Drain off all but ½ to 1 inch of drippings from Dutch oven. Spoon ⅓ of the Cherry Glaze on meat. Bake uncovered 30 minutes, spooning a small amount of glaze on meat every 10 minutes. Serve remaining glaze with meat.

Cherry Glaze

Combine 1 can (21 ounces) cherry pie filling, ¼ cup vinegar and ¼ teaspoon each salt, cinnamon, nutmeg and cloves in saucepan. Heat to boiling, stirring occasionally. Reduce heat; simmer 2 minutes. Keep warm over low heat while glazing meat.

POTATO POTS WITH PEAS 'N CARROTS

4 medium baking potatoes (about
    5 × 2½ inches)
1 cup frozen peas and carrots (about
    6 ounces)

Margarine
Salt and pepper

Heat 1 inch salted water (½ teaspoon salt to 1 cup water) to boiling in large saucepan. Add unpared potatoes; cover and heat to boiling. Reduce heat; simmer 20 minutes. Drain potatoes and peel. With melon ball cutter, scoop out centers of potatoes to form boat or bowl shapes (see note).

In deep fat fryer or kettle, heat 3 to 4 inches fat or oil to 370°. While oil is heating, cook frozen peas and carrots as directed on package; drain. Fry potato boats in hot fat until golden brown and thoroughly cooked, about 3 minutes; drain. (Unfilled potato boats can be kept warm on ungreased baking sheet in 140° oven 1 to 2 hours.) Brush cavities of potato boats with margarine; season with salt and pepper. Fill with hot peas and carrots.

Note: Mash the scooped-out portions of potatoes (1½ to 1¾ cups). Use in potato pancakes, potato refrigerator dough, creamy potato soup or vichyssoise.

GREENS WITH GARLIC CROUTONS

Garlic Croutons (below)
1 small head lettuce
1 green onion, chopped (with top)

1 stalk celery, thinly sliced
⅓ cup oil and vinegar dressing

Prepare Garlic Croutons. Tear lettuce into bite-size pieces (about 4 cups). Add onion, celery and dressing; toss until greens are coated. Sprinkle croutons on salad.

Garlic Croutons

Heat oven to 400°. Trim crusts from 4 slices white bread. Generously spread margarine on both sides of each slice; sprinkle both sides with garlic powder. Cut slices into ½-inch cubes and place in ungreased baking pan. Bake, stirring occasionally, until golden brown and crisp, 10 to 15 minutes.

CHOCOLATE PUFF DESSERT

½ angel food cake (10-inch size)
2 eggs, separated
¼ teaspoon cream of tartar
½ cup confectioners' sugar
¼ cup confectioners' sugar
¼ cup margarine, softened

1 ounce melted unsweetened chocolate (cool)
½ teaspoon vanilla
Dash salt
¼ cup chopped nuts

Tear cake into bite-size pieces. In small mixer bowl, beat egg whites and cream of tartar until foamy. Beat in ½ cup confectioners' sugar, 1 tablespoon at a time; beat until stiff and glossy. In another small mixer bowl, beat ¼ cup confectioners' sugar and the margarine until smooth and fluffy. Mix in egg yolks, chocolate, vanilla and salt on medium speed, scraping bowl occasionally.

Fold chocolate mixture into egg white meringue; stir in nuts. Fold in cake pieces until all are thoroughly coated. Turn into ungreased loaf pan, 9×5×3 inches. Refrigerate until set, at least 8 hours. Serve with whipped topping and garnish with maraschino cherries if you wish.   8 servings—refrigerate 4 servings for another meal.

FOR SIX
Crispy Chicken
Buttered Noodles
Crunchy Sprouts
Strawberry Cooler
or Strawberry Sundaes

CRISPY CHICKEN

¼ cup margarine	1 clove garlic, crushed
½ teaspoon celery salt	6 chicken legs (drumsticks and thighs)
¼ teaspoon ginger	2 cups chow mein noodles, coarsely crushed
1 teaspoon salt	

Heat oven to 350°. Melt margarine in baking pan, 13×9×2 inches; stir in celery salt, ginger, salt and garlic. Place chicken skin side down in margarine mixture; turn skin side up. Sprinkle chicken with noodles and press gently onto chicken. Bake uncovered until chicken is tender and golden brown, about 1½ hours.

CRUNCHY SPROUTS

2 pints Brussels sprouts (about 1½ pounds)	1 cup soft bread crumbs (about 4 slices)
2 tablespoons margarine	1 tablespoon lemon juice

Heat 1 inch salted water (½ teaspoon salt to 1 cup water) to boiling in saucepan. Add Brussels sprouts; cover and heat to boiling. Reduce heat; simmer until tender, 8 to 10 minutes.

While sprouts are cooking, melt margarine in small skillet over medium heat. Add bread crumbs and cook, stirring occasionally, until toasted and golden brown, about 5 minutes.

Drain Brussels sprouts; turn into serving dish. Sprinkle sprouts with lemon juice and top with bread crumbs.

STRAWBERRY COOLER

1 package (10 ounces) frozen sliced strawberries, partially thawed	3 cups vanilla ice cream, slightly softened
	1 cup milk

Mix all ingredients in blender or with electric mixer just until blended and thick. Cover; refrigerate until ready to serve. Serve in glasses or mugs.

Note: If you prefer to serve Strawberry Sundaes, just spoon thawed berries onto scoops of ice cream.

I NDEX